SIDNEY CROSBY

3rd Edition

J. Alexander Poulton

OVER
TIME
BOOKS

© 2011 by OverTime Books
First printed in 2011 10 9 8 7 6 5 4 3 2 1
Printed in Canada

The Publisher: OverTime Books is an imprint of Éditions de la Montagne Verte

Library and Archives Canada Cataloguing in Publication

Poulton, J. Alexander (Jay Alexander), 1977–
    Sidney Crosby / J. Alexander Poulton. — 3rd ed.

ISBN 978-1-897277-69-0

        1. Crosby, Sidney, 1987–. 2. Hockey players—Canada—Biography. 3. Pittsburgh Penguins (Hockey team)—Biography. 4. Cole Harbour (N.S.)—Biography. I. Title.

GV848.5.C76P69 2011   796.962092   C2011-900349-X

Project Director: J. Alexander Poulton
Project Editor: Kathy van Denderen
Cover Image: Courtesy of Corbis/Mike Cassese, photographer

PC: 1

Contents

A Journey to the 2008 Stanley Cup Playoffs

The last game of the 2007–08 season for the Pittsburgh Penguins saw them going up against the Philadelphia Flyers. A victory would assure the Penguins first place overall in the Eastern Conference, enabling them to jump past the Montreal Canadiens. But for some teams, finishing first is not always desirable.

During the regular season, the Pittsburgh Penguins lost the season series to the Ottawa Senators, but they had been without the services of Sidney Crosby, Gary Roberts and goalie Marc-Andre Fleury and could not withstand the Senators' potent offense. But in the final dozen games, the Senators were stricken with injuries to their top players and ended the season with a losing record. The Pens, on the other hand, regained the services of Crosby, Roberts and Fleury and put together an impressive end to the season, finishing with 102 points.

Come the final game, the Penguins must have secretly wished to face off against the Senators in the first round of the playoffs, but to do so they could not win the game against the Philadelphia Flyers. If they won, Pittsburgh would face the Flyers, a team that posed a much greater threat than the Senators. To get their dream first-round opponent, they needed the Flyers to do them a favor of sorts.

Watching the Penguins play the Flyers in their final game of the season, it seemed (though the players and the coach denied it vehemently) that the Pens were completely uninterested in winning the game. With one of the most potent offenses in the league and a solid defense, you might guess that the Pittsburgh Penguins could match any team in the league, but during the last game against the Flyers, they failed to pot a single goal and lost the game by a score of 2–0. The loss assured the Penguins that they would play the Senators in the first round.

For Pittsburgh Penguins captain Sidney Crosby, it was a chance at redemption. One year earlier, the two clubs had met in the first round of the 2007 playoffs, which just happened to be Crosby's first taste of playoff action, and the Senators unceremoniously took out the Pens in five games. Young Captain Sidney surely wanted some revenge.

The Senators limped into Pittsburgh's Mellon Arena without the essential services of their captain Daniel Alfredsson and the gritty Mike Fisher. Before they even stepped onto the ice, the Senators had a dark cloud over their heads from a season-opening high followed by a crushing finale.

The key for Pittsburgh would be the performance of their goaltender Marc-Andre Fleury and, of course, how Captain Crosby handled the pressure of his second foray into the Stanley Cup playoffs.

Everyone going into the series knew Ottawa's chances of winning were slim, but if they were to succeed, they needed the secondary scorers such as Antoine Vermette to step up, and they also needed their number one goaltender, Martin Gerber, to be the best player.

Unfortunately for Ottawa, however, their team was too broken to be fixed during the playoffs, and even the return of Alfredsson late in the series could do nothing to make them much of a challenge for the Penguins.

Sidney remained quiet in the first game, and still the Penguins won 4–0. Crosby came to life in the second game and burned the Senators with four assists in a Penguins' 5–3 victory. It would have been a much higher score in the game had it not been for Senators goalie Martin Gerber, who stood on his proverbial head, stopping 49 of 54 shots.

"Fifty-four shots? There's only so much a goaltender can do," Crosby said. "We were playing great hockey. When it was 3–3, we weren't happy, but we had to keep playing the way we were, and we got rewarded. We knew if we kept playing like that, we'd be fine."

In the third game, it was the Senators Nick Foligno who opened the scoring, but that was quickly put out by a goal by the Penguins Max Talbot, and Sidney Crosby potted his first playoff goal with a tie-breaker 11 seconds into the third period. The game ended with a final score of 4–1 (with additional Penguins goals by Jordan Staal and Marian Hossa), leaving Pittsburgh one win away from sweeping the series.

"It would be awesome, no question about it," Staal said. "It would be a little payback for last year. The fourth game is always the toughest to win, and we're going to have to come out with an even better effort than we did tonight."

Sidney and the Penguins came out with an even better effort in the fourth game, winning the game 4–1. The Penguins were the victors, and for Sidney the victory was sweet.

The Senators, who had started off the season with a 15–2 record, now were in the exact same place they had left the Penguins at around the same time in the 2007 playoffs. The irony was certainly not lost on Crosby.

"It feels great," Crosby said. "Obviously it was a different situation last year and we definitely went through some learning experiences there, but we responded well here in the first round. Most of us, our first playoff memory was losing here, so that's changed now."

Having broken the ice with a win over the Senators, the Pittsburgh Penguins confidence was at a season high and Sidney knew that this just might be the year that he got his chance at achieving his dream....

Chapter One

Winter Nights and Summer Days in Cole Harbour

Sidney's father Troy Crosby, like most Canadian boys, had dreamed of one day making it in the National Hockey League. He had put in the required hours of practice, made his way up through the minor league systems and was actually drafted by the Montreal Canadiens 240th overall in the 1984 Entry Draft (the Canadiens second goaltender draftee that year). Had Troy been drafted a year earlier, things might have worked out differently with the Canadiens, but the same year he was drafted, another goaltender by the name of Patrick Roy was also trying to work his way into the Canadiens organization. Troy Crosby had no chance of breaking into the league on the Canadiens squad, and after one more season with the Verdun Junior Canadiens, he called his hockey career quits and returned to his native Nova Scotia to start a family with his wife Trina.

Hockey and Nova Scotia have a long, illustrious history. It is in this scenic province on Canada's east coast that the elements of hockey first arose and spread out to the rest of the world. In the early 1800s, Thomas C. Haliburton, noted lawyer and man of letters, wrote one of the first descriptions of the game of hockey in his memoirs of his time at King's Preparatory School in Windsor, Nova Scotia:

"...and the school-room, and the noisy, larkin' happy holidays, and you boys let out racin', yelpin', hollerin', and whoopin' like mad with pleasure, and the play-ground, and the games at bass [base] in the fields, or hurly on the long pond on the ice."

Things haven't really changed all that much in some parts of the province, where on a cold winter morning boys still can be found "yelpin', hollerin', and whoopin' like mad with pleasure" as they play pick-up hockey on the local rinks. Hockey's ancestor, "hurling," was similar to the modern game today, except that hurling was played with more men on the ice and had far fewer rules.

Born on August 7, 1987, Sidney Crosby's odyssey into the world of hockey, unlike most hockey stories, did not begin on the ice, but in the basement of his parents' house in Cole Harbour, Nova

Scotia. Although his father put him in skates at the age of three, Sidney was not allowed into competitive hockey until he was five years old. This meant many days spent in the basement of his suburban home, honing the skills that would one day make him one of the best players in the game. It's not like there were other things to distract the young Crosby from his game; after all, Cole Harbour was hardly a hub of excitement. With nothing better to do, Sidney practiced hockey everywhere he could. He became so obsessed with the game that the woman who ran his daycare had to inform his parents that she could not play hockey with him every day and that she needed to attend to the other children. Sidney's parents attempted to distract him with other activities, but all he wanted to do was play hockey.

"When he was three or four, I bought him a toy gas station. He didn't play with that thing once. He would rather do something where he was competing. He always had a ton of energy," said Sidney's mother.

When Sidney couldn't play outside, he could usually be found in the basement, where his father had set up a piece of Plexiglas on the floor near the dryer so that Sidney could practice his shot. Not yet possessing perfect aim, he occasionally hit the dryer with the puck, which undoubtedly caught the attention of his parents upstairs. But after the millionth shot, both of them gave up any hope of rescuing their dryer and surrendered it to young Sidney for target practice. Sidney sometimes even dressed up his grandmother in whatever padding was available, with her permission, of course, and placed her in "nets" as goaltender. "She wasn't very old, and she played goalie and could move pretty well. I'd shoot on her, too." There was little doubt that young Sidney Crosby was obsessed with hockey.

If playing hockey was his first love, then watching hockey was surely his second. Every chance he got, Sidney would sprint to the television to see his hockey heroes, such as Wayne Gretzky, Steve Yzerman and Mario Lemieux. Crosby learned a lot from veteran players like Gretzky, studying his moves and dissecting how he approached each aspect of the game on the ice. Little did Sidney know that this was excellent training for a young hockey mind in development, to watch and retain the lessons of some of the game's greatest.

Countless hours spent in the basement, bashing up the dryer and shooting pucks at grandma, paid off when it finally came time for Sidney to strap on some pads and play competitive hockey.

Right from the start, his parents knew their innocent boy had a unique talent for the game. The fundamentals of the game came easily to Sidney, and soon after enrolling in his local team, he advanced much faster than the other children. Still oblivious to his raw talent, Sidney always tried to improve upon his game, and at night when he retreated to his room, covered in posters of players from his favorite team—the Montreal Canadiens—he would dream of one day making it into the big leagues, just like his heroes.

But like every superstar, you have to start somewhere, and one year after the Pittsburgh Penguins won their second Stanley Cup in a row, in 1992, and the NHL celebrated 75 years in existence, Troy Crosby took his son to the local arena and enrolled him with the Dartmouth Timbits hockey team. From the outset, everyone who witnessed Crosby play knew the kid had something special. Not only could he score goals and put up assists, but he also had that intangible quality that few players possess. Into his sixth year on the planet, young Sidney was already playing against players two or three years older than him, and he was still putting up fantastic numbers. Everywhere the young kid went, he garnered more and more attention.

In the summer of 1994, when he was seven years old, Sidney enrolled in a local hockey camp to learn a few new skills, and it was there that he met a 14-year-old from Murray Harbour, Prince Edward Island, named Brad Richards, who was hired to help train the kids. At 14 years of age, Richards was just starting to generate significant interest from central scouting, and an older Brad recalled seeing something special in Sidney at age seven. "You could see, even then, he was so much better than anyone else on the ice. He would go up against guys who were two, three years older than him and dominate."

Like most of the greats in the NHL, a common thread can be found in most of their stories. The stories of players like Gordie Howe, Rocket Richard, Bobby Orr and Wayne Gretzky do not differ all that much from Crosby's childhood in Cole Harbour. The most obvious connection between all the great players, whether they play hockey, baseball or basketball, is an incredible work ethic and a religious-like devotion to the game. As many hours as Crosby spent in his basement working on his aim, Gretzky spent just as many on his backyard rink. The countless times Crosby gave up pursuing other childhood activities, so did Gretzky. Hockey was the only thing that mattered to these youngsters.

The other important factor in producing a great hockey player is the role of the family, with an emphasis on the father. From the first tentative steps on the ice through the bumps and bruises of competitive hockey, to his son's rookie season in the NHL and beyond, Walter Gretzky was a fixture in Wayne's life, just as Troy Crosby is never too far from his son. Sidney Crosby and Wayne Gretzky have the natural talent for hockey, but it only blossomed into something greater because of the constant support system they could always rely on through the good and the bad times. It is that kind of support system that makes players like Gretzky and Crosby great players on the ice; and off the ice, it makes them incredibly nice, salt-of-the-earth people.

The one part of Sidney's story that doesn't follow the others, however, is that he grew up in Halifax. Nothing against the wonderful city, but a kid growing up in that part of Nova Scotia does not have much access to good ice. With the city's temperate climate, outdoor arenas are few and far between, and the ones that are around are often unplayable. Crosby never had the archetypical backyard hockey rink or access to a frozen pond. He had to hone his skills in a much different manner, and for that he gives his grandmother many thanks.

Like the Gretzkys before them, the Crosbys knew their son was special. As Troy Crosby once told a reporter from the *Globe and Mail*, "He was doing a lot of things naturally. Kids that age want to carry the puck from one end of the ice to the other to score. Even at six, Sidney was a natural passer. Stuff like that is not normal." This innate ability for the game was not only noticed by his proud parents but also by every single person who witnessed what he could do on the ice. When Sidney was seven years old, the local newspaper even came calling and did a story on the young phenom. But for all the attention, Sidney remained a kid who loved to play hockey and wanted to be the best. As he got older, he began to show more and more people how good he was and could become.

Enrolled in the atom league in Cole Harbour, Sidney proceeded to garner even more attention by recording 159 goals and 121 assists, for an amazing total of 280 points in 55 games. This worked out to about an average of more than five points per game over the season. Although this made Sidney's parents and teammates happy, many of the other parents and officials weren't excited by the presence of the young star in the making.

At a meeting of the Cole Harbour Hockey Association when Crosby was 12 years old, it was decided that it was best for all interested parties if he were not allowed to play in any league in advance of his age. Similar to skipping a grade, playing in higher leagues is a hot topic among the 5:00 AM Tim Hortons' crowd. Moving a child ahead is often viewed upon as being the overly proud ambitions of hockey parents rather than the specific needs of the young hockey player, but in Sidney's case he was not any ordinary hockey player. For most of his young hockey career he was playing against boys who were two or three years older than him, and he was still the best player.

Sidney was set to play a game for the Cole Harbour Red Wings bantam AAA team in a tournament where a 12-year-old would look a little conspicuous standing next to 15-year-olds in a league that allowed full body contact. The question wasn't whether Crosby's skill level could match up with the older players but whether some of the 6-foot-tall 15-year-olds would hurt him. With Sidney's health and well-being in mind, the local hockey association decided to bar him from playing in the bantams. But the coach of the Cole Harbour Red Wings, Harry O'Donnell, had other plans. He wanted a win, and he knew the best way to do that was to put Crosby on the ice. And for that decision O'Donnell received a one-game suspension.

"I knew that I would get spanked for it, but I didn't expect this. I just wanted to put the best players on the ice...that's the bottom line. They (the Cole Harbour Hockey Association) didn't agree...," O'Donnell told a reporter from the *Halifax Daily News*. "What would have happened to Wayne Gretzky if they did that to him?"

The association only saw a kid standing 5 foot 2 and weighing 110 pounds soaking wet, who would not be able to survive in an arena full of boys the size of NHLers. It didn't matter that Sidney never once objected to playing, had proven himself in other full contact games and, despite all the odds against him, had scored one goal and three assists in the tournament to give the victory to the Cole Harbour Red Wings squad. If the association was so worried about the welfare of Sidney, they might have investigated further into his actual play on the ice. They would have found that of all the guys he played against, not one of them noticed his "small" size. Every time he stepped out onto the ice, Sidney gave a complete effort and was often stronger on his skates than players twice his size. But after that one game, Sidney was banned from playing in the higher levels and was sent back down to play with kids his own age. What might have seemed a minor disagreement between parents and a hockey association turned out to be headline news in the local paper, and caught in the middle was a little boy who just wanted to play hockey.

"I think it's pretty cheap, because Brent Theriault (another peewee playing up in the league) will be playing for the Halifax Hawks, and I can't play. I wanted to finish my season this weekend playing in the Bantam Atlantics, but now I can't. It's just politics, I guess," Sidney told the *Halifax Daily News*.

Troy Crosby tried appealing to the Cole Harbour Hockey Association, but they didn't return his phone calls. He wanted the best for his son, but many parents saw this as Troy favoring his child's development over others. This often left cold feelings in the already icy air at the local arenas. Trina and Troy attempted to shield their son from all the drama, but he could never be kept completely isolated and had to build a tough skin early on in his career to handle the countless verbal attacks from players and parents alike. But instead of getting angry about the abuse and retreating from the pressure, Sidney had his own way of exacting revenge, by hitting the opposition where it hurt the most, on the scoreboard.

Being sent back down to his age level really only delayed the inevitable. Although Sidney continued to post incredible numbers, he was still just a local celebrity of sorts among the hockey crowd, and it wasn't until he turned 14 that the name Sidney Crosby turned up on everywhere.

Chapter Two

Coming Out of the Dark

It is a familiar story in Canada to attach so much promise to a young player only to have him fail when he reaches the higher levels of the game. Look no further than Alexandre Daigle. Like Crosby, Daigle was a highly touted junior, but when he made the jump to the big leagues with the Ottawa Senators in 1994, he did not make the impact the Senators were hoping for. For those who watched the development of Sidney Crosby, many doubted that he could make it outside of the East Coast hockey circles, given that the Halifax area does not have a remarkable history for producing high-quality players (Al MacInnis of Inverness, Nova Scotia, excluded). Questions surrounded Sidney that he might have been the top player in his market, but placed up against teams from Toronto, Montreal or Edmonton, he might not fair as well. If he was to be anointed the next Great One, he needed to prove himself against the higher level of talent from across Canada.

At 14 years old, Sidney was tearing up the midget AAA level with the Dartmouth Subways, scoring 193 points in just 74 games, and he even played a few games with the Truro Bearcats of the Maritime Junior A Hockey League. His scoring prowess and leadership abilities helped propel the Subways to the provincial championship and to qualify for Canada's top midget tournament, the Air Canada Cup, by winning the Atlantic regional tournament. In the lead-up to the Air Canada tournament, Sidney was by far the most standout player on any of the teams, and a definite buzz surrounded the northern New Brunswick town of Bathurst before any of the games even began.

This was Sidney's moment to shine. It was the first real tournament where the country would see Canada's best young talent, and as Peter Assaff of the *Northern Light* newspaper put it, "The city was already very excited about hosting the National Championships. But when word got around that Sidney Crosby was coming to town to play, the excitement and anticipation rose to another level."

Ever since he was about seven years old, Sidney had caused a certain buzz around him, and the Air Canada Cup tournament was his chance to prove to doubters that his skills could withstand the physical and emotional pressure of a major tournament against Canada's best. Although we all know now what kind of player Sidney Crosby turned out to be, back when he was 14, he was 5 foot 8 and weighed 165 pounds, not the most dominating physical presence on the ice when up against players who were upwards of 6 feet tall and 200 pounds. He had played against guys much bigger than him for most of his brief hockey career, but this tournament was his biggest challenge. In the weeks leading up to the tournament, you had to be living in a bubble to not have heard the hype surrounding the arrival of Sidney Crosby, and his opposition was more than aware that if they wanted to beat the Dartmouth Subways, containing Sidney would be the key. But questions kept coming up about his size. Remember, this was prior to the lockout season of 2004–05 when most teams were actively looking for big impact players. Most kids being drafted into the NHL at that time were over 6 feet tall and hovered around 200 pounds—next to Sidney, they all looked like giants. Hockey was the domain of the big boy, and people wondered whether Sidney's talent would translate into the "big" leagues. The task would not be easy, but if Crosby could put some significant numbers on the board despite the constant attention, then he would certainly solidify his status as a star in the making. If the bigger players succeeded in containing him, all his critics would be proven correct, and his stock as a future NHLer would certainly plummet.

The hockey game finally got underway. Sidney knew that he would get most of the attention, but that did not deter him one bit from sticking to his game. Opposing teams tried, and on some shifts succeeded in shutting him down, but it was next to impossible to contain him for the entire game, and when someone missed their assignment, Sidney made them pay. He led the Subways through the preliminaries and into the elimination rounds as the competition picked up. The ice got smaller, and the players got rougher, but Sidney never backed down. The 6-foot tall, 200-pound players quickly discovered what all the hype was about.

In the first game it was clear that Crosby was the target, but it did little to affect his game overall. The mark of true champions is that when pushed, they push back harder, and Sidney never gave up. Players two or three years older and much bigger were able to check him a little harder, but when it came to battling for the puck, no one was stronger on the ice than Crosby.

Bigger players had an incredibly difficult time knocking Crosby off the puck. Because while many players focus on developing overall physical strength, it was and still remains part of Crosby's training practices to work on building lower body strength and cardio conditioning.

The first game of the tournament saw Crosby's Team Atlantic Dartmouth Subways up against the Pacific representatives, the Red Deer Chiefs. Players, coaches, fans and parents knew it was going to be a rough game as the Chiefs played a hard and fast style of hockey that took no prisoners. And their game plan was simple—stop Crosby.

"Everyone in the building, including Crosby, knew what Red Deer's game plan would be. Nail Crosby at every turn, and make him a non-issue in the game," noted Subways coach Brad Crossley.

Right from the first drop of the puck it was almost comical to watch as wave after wave of Red Deer players tried to contain Crosby, sometimes double-teaming him, but somehow Sid the Kid managed to get away. The players were so focused on stopping Crosby that when he avoided the checking, no one was in position to stop him from going to the net. He thoroughly embarrassed the Red Deer game plan by scoring a natural hat trick and adding two assists in the first period alone to give the Subways a 5–0 lead. The first-period beating the Chiefs took at the hands of Crosby seemed to spark them back to life, and they came out flying in the second. Taking him out of their heads for the rest of the game, the Chiefs were able to mount a comeback and defeat the Subways by a final score of 8–6. As much as the crowd was sad to see the Subways lose, all everyone could talk about afterwards was the performance of Sidney Crosby. In the first game of the tournament, with the eyes of the nation on him—and every Red Deer Chief out to knock him out cold—he rose above expectations and put in one of the best performances of the tournament. Luckily, this was just a round-robin match, and Crosby soon got his revenge.

Through each game, Sidney Crosby did not let down his team or his fans, leading the Subways through the preliminaries and into the elimination rounds. All the critics were quickly jumping on the Crosby bandwagon as shift after shift he put on an MVP performance. He was not only scoring goals, but his win-at-all-costs attitude also made sure that everyone on the team got their fair share of tape-to-tape passes. His skills on the ice helped to lift the team into the semifinals, back up against their Pacific rivals, the Red Deer Chiefs.

Crosby put in another all-star performance during the game, taking extreme abuse from the Chiefs' defensive specialists every time he stepped onto the ice, but he still remained active in the game, ever the scoring threat. The score was tied 3–3 in the dying seconds of the third period, and it was Sidney Crosby who came to the rescue of his teammates. He scored the decisive power-play maker, sending his team into the finals of the Air Canada Cup to face Saskatchewan's Tisdale Trojans.

Unfortunately for Crosby, the tournament did not turn out the way he had hoped. In the championship game, the Subways could not find a rhythm and looked nervous every time they took possession of the puck. The championship jitters led to a few Subway errors, and by the end of the first period, Sidney and his team were down 3–0. The only highlight for the Subways came in the second period when a teammate hit Crosby with a perfect pass as he was streaking through center ice, and with a nice deke, Crosby put his team on the board. But that wasn't enough to spark a comeback, and the Dartmouth Subways had to settle for the Air Canada Cup consolation prize, a silver medal.

"They definitely caught us by surprise. We were a little nervous at the start and we didn't get our feet moving. We might have been a little bit tentative playing in front of a national television audience, but we can't use that as an excuse. They beat us and they're a great team," said a humbled Crosby to a swarm of reporters after the game.

Despite losing the game championship, Crosby received individual recognition for his outstanding play during the Air Canada Cup and was named the tournament's most valuable player. There were other quality players in the tournament, but it was hard to overlook a player who scored 11 goals and 13 assists in seven games— and who was only 14 years old.

Even the opposing players knew who the star of the tournament was. During the post-game handshake, Tisdale captain Michael Olson told Crosby, "You're a hell of a hockey player, and I'll probably be watching you some day on TV." Crosby had earned the respect he deserved but almost certainly would have rather had the championship instead.

This was the first time an Atlantic team had made it into the finals in the tournament's 24-year history, gaining a huge amount of respect for an eastern hockey program that was often said to be weak and irrelevant in producing quality hockey players. At 14 years of age, Crosby had conquered the midget ranks, and he now sought out a new challenge.

Chapter Three

New Territory

After dominating at the 2002 Air Canada Cup, Sidney Crosby needed a new challenge. Still 14 in the summer of 2002, he needed to make a decision about where he was going to play hockey. But as he had already conquered the Atlantic hockey program, Crosby's only other option was to seek out new challenges and leave the comforts of Cole Harbour, Nova Scotia.

It was a tough decision, something most NHL players have to make at some point in their early careers when the local hockey being offered wasn't meeting the challenge they needed for their burgeoning talent. Even the Great One himself, Wayne Gretzky, had to leave the security of his childhood home in Brampton, Ontario, for the opportunity to play in Toronto's minor system. Although it comforted Crosby to know that countless other hockey players had gone through the same experience, it didn't make the decision any easier, but the choice had to be made. The only problem was to find somewhere to play.

As in the past, Sidney faced another roadblock because of his age. It was obvious to anyone who had seen him play that Crosby was ready to make the leap into the major junior ranks. However, the major junior's did not allow any player under the age of 16, and Sidney was 15. Exceptions had been made in the past. Gare Joyce, in his biography of Sidney Crosby, states the example of Jason Spezza and John Tavares who, both at 15, were granted permission to play in the Ontario Hockey League (OHL). Most believed Sidney Crosby was a prospect of equal or greater value, so it only seemed fair that whatever major junior league he wanted to enter would grant him special status.

However, that was not the case. The Quebec Major Junior Hockey League (QMJHL) held firm in its stance on not allowing Crosby to play in the league. The official reason for the ban was that he was not old enough, and that if they continued to make exceptions, then players in the future with less skill than Crosby would one day try to follow. But the truth was that Crosby's most likely destination would be the QMJHL Halifax Mooseheads, and seeing as they were already one of the stronger and richer teams, the other team executives expressed serious concerns about giving the Mooseheads an obvious advantage. But as Gare Joyce points out, the league almost certainly denied itself a considerable gate attraction no matter which team Crosby played for. Despite the repeated requests to make one last exception, the QMJHL held their ground, leaving Crosby with only two options on where to pursue his development.

It truly was a case of finding the right fit to develop Crosby's game even further. Watching Crosby play, it was easy to forget he was 15 years old and had many things to learn before he could move up in the hockey ranks. What he needed from the next stage of his hockey development was an environment that could provide him with a challenging hockey climate and a place to grow as a man. After the Air Canada Cup, Crosby informed reporters of his choices. "I'm not sure I'm going to prep school or play junior A. Those are the only two things I can do, and I'm not really sure yet, " he said.

Junior A presented a few problems, however. Although he would have the pool of talent that he needed to push him to new levels, the media attention and scrutiny he would be under most certainly would distract him from his intended goal. After much discussion with his family, Crosby decided to go the route of the prep school. Shattuck-St. Mary's proved to be the perfect fit. The Minnesota private school had only 300 students, was far away from the media attention he would receive in Canada and for some time had been drawing some of the best talent from the United States and Canada. Shattuck was an ideal place for Crosby to get all that he needed professionally and personally.

A major factor in Crosby's selection of Shattuck as his destination had to be the involvement of former Minnesota North Star and member of Team Canada during the 1972 Summit Series, J.P. Parise. As the school's program director, Parise had built a solid reputation for developing young talent and had received top marks for working with players who were considered "undersized," like his own son, NHLer Zach Parise. For Sidney, leaving his parents was tough, but getting out of arenas in eastern Canada was the perfect fit for the whole family.

"I remember the day when the Crosbys made the decision on Shattuck," family friend Ed Spidel explained in Gare Joyce's book. "I remember Trina just being so relieved that it was over and done with. She was going to miss Sidney, and he was going to miss his parents and Taylor (his little sister). But things were getting tougher for Troy and Trina at the arenas. There were a lot of demands on them. There was a lot of attention. And some people just said awful things to them and to Sidney. Another season, especially after all the success that the Subways had at the Air Canada Cup, was going to be too much for them."

But before heading off to Minnesota, Sidney finally got to enjoy the perks of being such a well-recognized player. In July 2002 his managing agency, IMG, asked him to fly to Los Angeles, where IMG's top clients were being showcased in a development camp and where the future stars were given the chance to skate alongside players with considerable NHL experience. One of those players in attendance was Wayne Gretzky. He had heard a few things about Sidney through the hockey grapevine, but nothing that he hadn't heard before. However, this was the first time the "Great One" would get a chance to see "the Next One" in action. Gretzky had said upon his retirement that it was the last time he would wear a pair of skates, but when he saw Sidney on the ice, he had to join him for a few drills. After a few paces with the kid, Gretzky was impressed, and impressing Gretzky is no easy task. Gretzky spoke to Gare Joyce about that memorable day when the two hockey players met.

"He saw everything on the ice. He saw the game the same way I did when I was 14. He just had these incredible skills and a real love of the game—an incredible desire to do whatever it takes to be better. He's the best talent to come along since Mario and what makes him different is the attention to conditioning and work in the gym," said Gretzky.

Such high praise for a 14-year-old, made all the more astounding given that it came from the legend, Wayne Gretzky. At the end of the 2002–03 NHL season, a reporter asked Gretzky if anyone in the modern NHL would ever have a chance at beating his records. Only one player (who was not in the NHL and not even allowed to drive) came to his mind. "Sidney Crosby. He's dynamite." Gretzky also added in another interview that if there was any other player out there who could break some of his seemingly unbreakable records, it was Sidney Crosby.

Sidney was extremely flattered by the sudden praise from Gretzky. "I realize there will not be another Gretzky, and I will be the first one to say I will not break his records. But for him to say that I could, means I'm doing something right. It was probably the best compliment I could get. I'm going to remember it for a long time."

As if such high praise from Gretzky wasn't enough to stimulate a young hockey fan's mind, before leaving for Shattuck, Hockey Canada invited Sidney to be the stick boy at the under-20 team's evaluation camp for the World Junior Championship held in Halifax and (strangely enough) Sydney, Nova Scotia. It was meant to be a learning experience for the young Crosby, an opportunity to hang around players who were as highly touted as he was, such as Jason Spezza and Marc-Andre Fleury. Sidney tried to soak up as much information as he could and enjoyed every minute he spent in the program. Sidney was even on the bench as Canada made its way through the preliminaries and into the finals, only to watch them lose 3–2 to the Russians and leader Alexander Ovechkin. Sidney would soon have his own chance on the ice wearing the Team Canada colors.

With dreams of a bigger and better future ahead, Sidney arrived at Shattuck ready to play, and after only a few games playing with the Shattuck-St. Mary's Sabres, he confirmed that everyone had made the right decision. Teamed up with hockey prodigies Jack Johnson and Drew Stafford, Crosby helped the Sabres to one of their most impressive starts in franchise history. Traveling throughout the United States and Canada, Crosby and the Sabres finished the

2002–03 season with one of their best records in years. Crosby played in 57 games and scored 72 goals and 90 assists for 162 points. (Drew Stafford came in second place in team-scoring, 50 points behind Sidney.) As the team rolled into the playoffs, Sidney anticipated that yet again he would be the opposition's main target. But as he had always shown throughout his hockey development, when pushed, he played even better.

Up against the Eastern Massachusetts Senators in the first round, Sidney and the Sabres prepared for an intense battle. The Senators were the biggest competition the Sabres had, and playing them in the opening of the playoff rounds was a good test for the team. As predicted, the Senators went after Crosby at every opportunity but were continually frustrated by his ability to fight off a checker and get himself out into the open. Led by Sidney, the Sabres quickly dispensed of the Senators and moved on towards their ultimate target.

Next up were the Little Caesars from Detroit, Michigan, and the Midget Tier 1 Stars from Dallas, Texas. Both teams came in with the hopes of shutting down Crosby, and both were taken out of the playoffs for implementing the wrong strategy. The Sabres were into the final, up against the formidable Team Illinois. Illinois had just coming off a gold medal victory earlier in the season at the prestigious Mac Midget Hockey Tournament in Calgary, Alberta, and were looking to add to their collection.

The game was a battle, with the decision going down to the final seconds. With the Sabres up by two goals in the few remaining minutes, Team Illinois pulled their goaltender and managed to get within one, but time ran out on their hope of bringing another trophy back to Illinois as Sidney and the Sabres held on for the 5–4 victory and the league championship.

Finally, Sidney Crosby had the proof that he could lead a team to victory, by his individual efforts and by simply making everyone else around him better. After such a successful season, Sidney was now the number one prospect going into the 2003 QMJHL draft.

Chapter Four

Taking Rimouski by Storm

When the Rimouski Oceanic found out they had the number one pick overall at the 2003 Quebec Major Junior Hockey League (QMJHL) draft, there must have been a party in the team's executive boardroom. Sidney Crosby was on the menu, and the franchise was salivating at the prospect.

This was a prospect the Oceanic was hoping for. The Rimouski team had long been struggling in the QMJHL and needed a superstar to take them out of the basement of the league. In the 2003–04 season, the Oceanic had a paltry record of 11–58, the worst in the league. Not too long in their past, however, Rimouski had been a happy place. They had finished the season at the top of the league, had an exciting line-up of young talent (including Brad Richards, who Sidney had met a few years earlier at a hockey camp) and had the Memorial Cup Championship to show for all their hard work. But Brad Richards was called up to the NHL, and the team's fortunes seemed to follow him. Each season got progressively worse, and by 2002–03, the Oceanic were treading water. Fans weren't happy, players weren't happy, and most certainly the team's pockets weren't happy either. Thankfully, everything was about to change.

Crosby's coronation as the number one pick, however, was still in question. Sidney had a choice to make about his future, and he had an abundant number of places to choose from, in both Canada and the United States. Going the route of the U.S. college hockey program was a distinct possibility for him as it had a solid reputation, and he could continue to evolve, away from the prying eyes of the Canadian media. But Canadian major junior hockey still was the best place for producing talent and offering the biggest challenge to an athlete looking to test his skills. In the end, the Oceanic breathed a sigh of relief; Sidney Crosby would not be returning to the United States.

Entering the QMJHL was something Crosby did for his own benefit, but the league needed him more than he needed them. The league, or "the Q" as it is more commonly referred to, was not generally known as the hotbed of talent in the wider Canadian Hockey League. Historically, its players were less likely to be selected to represent Canada at international tournaments, and it was often the last stop for scouts. To say the league needed Crosby in 2003 was an understatement. Players like Brad Richards and Vincent Lecavalier had all been through the Q, but Crosby was a whole other level of superstar.

On draft day there really wasn't any suspense in the air that hinted how the draft would unfold. Crosby walked into the draft on Saturday, June 7, 2003, at the Palais des Sports in Val-d'Or, Quebec, with all eyes on him. The QMJHL president walked up to the microphone and announced the start of the draft. A delegation from Rimouski Oceanic crowded the stage, each person grinning from ear to ear. They walked up to the microphone and, to no one's surprise, called out the name of Sidney Crosby.

The history of the Rimouski franchise was one of serious ups and downs. When they first entered the Q in 1995, they were not the worst in the league, but they were not the best either. But over the years, by drafting players such as Vincent Lecavalier, J.P. Dumont, Mike Ribeiro, Brad Richards and Simon Gamache, the Oceanic went from bottom-feeders to Memorial Cup Champions. Yet as fast as their rise to the championship was, they just as quickly tumbled back down into the basement of the league. Draft picks were not working out, attendance began to decline, and the future was not looking bright. Getting Sidney Crosby would, on and off the ice, turn around the franchise.

Crosby was itching to get on the ice to see what kind of hockey he would face. He expected fast-paced and rough hockey, and that was exactly what he got. But if he was at all worried about his points production in the new league (he probably wasn't), he didn't have to wait long to adjust to the new style of play and show the fans that hockey had returned to Rimouski. In the four pre-season games alone, Crosby registered an incredible 14 points. Rimouski executives were very pleased with their new acquisition.

In the season opener, the Oceanic traveled to the tiny Quebec town of Rouyn-Noranda to play the Huskies. In the opening two periods Sidney watched as his new team fell behind in the game 3–1, and he did not like what he saw. In the third period, he decided to take control of the game and proceeded to score three goals in a row, leading his team to a 4–3 victory. For his efforts he received the game's first star and the immediate respect of his teammates. A few days later, the

Crosby show arrived back in Rimouski for the home opener, and a large crowd had already taken their seats before the game started. Fans got their money's worth and more as Sidney registered a five-point night, leading his team to victory over the Moncton Wildcats. In dramatic fashion, he assisted on the game-tying goal in the final minute of regulation and scored the winner in overtime all on his own, only nine seconds into the period. The team was flooded with orders for tickets and Oceanic jerseys with Crosby's name stitched on their backs.

By November, more and more hockey fans had begun to hear the name of Sidney Crosby across Canada and the United States, but on November 28, 2003, Crosby did something to ensure everyone knew his name.

That November day, the Quebec Remparts rolled into Rimouski to play their third game of the season against the team. The Remparts hadn't had any luck against the Oceanic all season, and this game was no different, as Sidney and his team took a commanding 3–0 lead by the end of the first period. It was during this game that Sidney decided to try something he had never done; something that he had only dared to try in practice. But when the opportunity arose in the game against the Remparts, he could not resist the temptation. At the start of the third period, when behind the Remparts net, he quickly flipped the puck onto the blade of his stick so that it lay flat and then wrapped his stick around the net and put the puck past the Remparts' goaltender while it was still on his stick. Elated at having scored the cool-looking goal, Crosby jumped up and down and celebrated as if he had just scored the overtime goal in the seventh game of the Stanley Cup finals. The goal was truly something to celebrate, but his antics on the ice that day upset a few people, and one person in particular.

Don Cherry, known as the protector of everything sacred in and around the game of hockey, was less than impressed with the young phenom. During one of his weekly tirades on the CBC's *Hockey Night in Canada* "Coach's Corner" program, Cherry spent a few minutes berating Crosby for his antics. "I like the kid," said Cherry while the playback of the goal rolled on screen. "But this is a hot dog move…the Quebec Remparts are going to remember that the next time they play. He's gonna get hurt. They're gonna grab the mustard and put it all over him." "Coach's Corner" co-host Ron MacLean tried to soften the obvious blow, but Cherry's comment had already reached too many ears to retract.

The 16-year-old Sidney Crosby, who wanted nothing more than to play hockey and score goals, was now the focus of nationwide media attention because Don Cherry used Canada's most popular show to blast Crosby for his show-manship. Canadians from coast to coast were quick to weigh in on the whole affair, and most were on the side of the young hockey player.

Radio shows and newspaper editorials were quick to defend Crosby, and they berated the elder TV host for using his power to attack a 16-year-old for doing what he does best. There were calls to boycott Cherry's show, and countless others poked fun at Cherry's unique choice of clothing. Cherry's comment caused such an uproar in the media that he was forced to address the issue on the next broadcast of *Hockey Night in Canada*. But he did not repent. "People reacted like I said something about the Pope." Not content with letting the issue go, Cherry tried to justify his comments but only dug the hole deeper by saying that he only singled Crosby out "to warn the kid about what can happen." He then backed his case by airing an interview with Detroit's Brendan Shanahan who, commenting on Crosby's goal, said that he would be "looking to take the head off" any player who dared pull off the same thing as Crosby. As if that wasn't enough, Cherry then laced into Crosby's parents.

"His parents evidently don't know anything about that stuff," said Cherry confidently. "Someone should have told him not to do it."

The goal, however, was not the first of its kind. Sidney, like many others, had seen the video of Mike Legg from the Michigan Wolverines score exactly the same way back in 1996. To Sidney, the whole affair was a little silly, and he just wanted to move on from the incident.

The affair finally died down when Sidney received an invitation to play at the Under-18 World Junior Championship in Finland.

Because Crosby was 16 years old, Hockey Canada had some reservations about inviting such a young player, since they had only done it four times in the past (Wayne Gretzky, Eric Lindros, Jason Spezza and Jay Bouwmeester), but this was Sidney Crosby, and he had been exceeding expectations all his life. This was an extremely special moment, and he was going to prove to everyone, yet again, that he deserved to be there. After training camp, he was happy to find out that his name was still on the roster list and that he was not going home early.

Sidney's family made the journey to Finland, and for the first game against the host country, brought a banner that was signed by hundreds of

Cole Harbour residents who were sending Sidney their good wishes. Unfortunately, in the first game, Sidney did not play much. For the first time in his life he wasn't the best player on the ice, but he tried hard every chance he got and made a good impression on the coaching staff. Sidney was more than content to be there and to get to play with such high-caliber players as Dion Phaneuf, Jeff Carter and future teammate Marc-Andre Fleury. It was in the next game against Switzerland that Sidney would step up his game and make history.

The game was not the biggest challenge for the Team Canada squad, and by late in the third period, Canada racked up an easy 6–2 lead. With only one minute remaining in the game, the coach sent Crosby out onto the ice, and Crosby took the opportunity to become the youngest player in World Junior Championship hockey to score a goal when he put a high shot past Swiss goaltender Daniel Manzato to give Team Canada a 7–2 victory. After potting another goal in their next game against the Ukraine, Crosby then showed everyone how good he could be in the final round-robin game against the strong Czech Republic.

Sidney left a few jaws on the floor when he helped to open the scoring with a pretty play.

Forcing a turnover in the Czech zone, he picked up the loose puck and fired a beautiful pass between two surprised Czech d-men onto the stick of Jeff Tambellini, who simply redirected the puck past the Czech goaltender. Using the first goal as motivation, Canada roared on to a 5–2 victory.

Team Canada made it through the playoff elimination rounds and into the finals against the United States, but unfortunately did not leave with the gold medal. Although Sidney had to settle for the silver, he took away an invaluable experience that he would later draw upon at future international events.

"Ever since the game ended, next year is all I've been thinking about. That feeling you have after losing is not fun. You want to make sure you don't have that again," said Crosby at the end of the tournament.

With the incredible experience of playing at the World Junior Championship at the young age of 16, Sidney returned to Rimouski to take back his place as the top scorer in the league, despite missing one month of games. It seemed that with each game he played, Sidney did something new that completely amazed everyone watching, and more and more people were going to QMJHL games just to see him play.

The Quebec Remparts sold out their stadium on a cold February night in 2005 when Sidney and the Oceanic rolled into town. Some 15,333 fans came out to support their team, but most were also curious to see the young hockey prodigy who everybody was talking about. Rimouski Oceanic jerseys with Crosby's now famous number 87 began to follow the team everywhere.

Game after game, goal after goal was added to Sidney's point totals. After playing in 59 games, he scored a team-leading 54 goals and 81 assists for a total of 135 points. That's an average of 2.2 points per game! Finishing the season with 76 points, the Oceanic was poised to make a serious run in the playoffs for the first time since their Memorial Cup win in 2000, something Crosby was relishing after losing the gold medal at the World Junior's.

But beforehand, he took a short break to collect a few honors from the QMJHL at the annual awards ceremony. It was almost a virtual sweep. He took home the top rookie, top rookie scorer, top scorer overall, most valuable player and the Paul Dumont Trophy. "There isn't a word in English for the Dumont. It's the award for the player who brings the most sunshine to the league," Rimouski official Yannick Dumais attempted to explain. It seemed the only trophy Crosby didn't win was the one for best goaltender.

After he got all the official stuff out of the way, Crosby focused on his real goal—winning the league championship and taking the team all the way to the Memorial Cup. But first he had to get by the Shawinigan Cataractes. Luckily the Cataractes were not the best team in the league, and Crosby helped his team defeat them in four games straight. Crosby did his part, scoring six times and helping out with six assists. But one goal stood out from the rest. In game two, Sidney was having a spectacular night. He had already potted two goals, which helped his team to an early 4–0 lead by the middle of the second period. However, it was his third of the night that had people talking.

After taking two penalties, Crosby was thrown on the ice to defend against the five-on-three Shawinigan attack. Looking to get back into the game, the Cataractes passed the puck around, looking for the perfect open opportunity, and when their defense made one too many cute passes, Crosby snatched the puck and bolted towards the opposition goaltender. With just a few strides of his skates, Crosby was completely out of reach of the stunned Shawinigan defense and headed in on the lone goalie. The home crowd jumped to their feet, excitedly anticipating Crosby's next move as he crossed the blue line. They were not disappointed. Crosby laid down an incredible deke moving to his backhand and pushing the puck past the dumbstruck Cataractes goaltender Julien Ellis-Plante. Sidney was as shocked as the fans, and though he had wanted to celebrate the goal with his teammates, none of them had made it to center ice by the time he had scored.

"I've never scored three-on-five before. Strangest thing is, after this goal, I threw up my arms and stood behind the net. I was looking for a teammate to celebrate with. The nearest one was at the other end of the ice, a hundred feet away. I had to skate all the way back to the bench alone," recounted Crosby later.

He hoped he could do the same kind of thing against the next team.

However, that team would be a little more of a challenge. While the Oceanic finished with 76 points, the Moncton Wildcats were in a class far above, with 96 points. The Wildcats did not have the scoring talent that the Oceanic possessed, but they allowed few chances in front of the net because of a really solid defensive squad.

In the first game of the series, Crosby opened up the scoring in the beginning of the second period, but that was all the offense the Oceanic could muster. Opposing teams had made Sidney Crosby their target and failed, but this time around the Wildcats' defense proved successful. The Wildcats scored four unanswered goals as they went on to win game one by a score of 4–1.

In game two, the Oceanic fared a little better and came out with a 2–1 victory, with Sidney assisting on both goals. But this was the only win the Wildcats allowed, and they won the series four games to one. The Wildcats learned that if you took Sidney Crosby out of the game, then the Oceanic did not have much of an offense to mount a significant attack. Sidney finished the series with just one goal and two assists.

Although the season didn't end the way he had hoped, somewhere deep inside, Crosby was surely pleased with his progress. After all, he had blown away all competition on an individual level, had received nationwide attention for his goal-scoring prowess and had become the youngest player ever to score a goal at the World Junior Championship. All eyes were on Sidney Crosby, and NHL teams were frothing at the mouth to get a chance at drafting the young superstar in the making.

But before the NHL could sink their teeth into the kid, he still had one more year of junior hockey to play, and when all was said and done, the Crosby brand would be the biggest that hockey had ever seen. With words of praise coming from the mouths of people like Wayne Gretzky, Sidney Crosby at age 17 was probably the most famous hockey player *not* in the NHL. Truly, what 17-year-old could say that he had been profiled in the pages of *Sports Illustrated* and *ESPN* magazine and had countless hours of radio and television broadcasts devoted to his singular talent? Surely, Gretzky would have had this much attention had he been born around the same time as Crosby, but this was a new era, and Crosby had the global media's spotlight all to himself. Long before he had even dreamed of putting on a NHL sweater, Sidney Crosby had already become a brand name. What made him such a valuable asset to hockey was not just that he could put incredibly high numbers on the board (in the prettiest way possibly) but that he remained a genuinely nice person and someone who simply played hockey for the love of it. That kind of player only comes along once in a generation, and since Gretzky had retired, hockey was in desperate need of someone like Sidney Crosby.

"He's down to earth for a kid being tagged with the label of the next Gretzky. He's an even better person than he is a player," said friend Zach Parise.

At the time that Crosby finished his rookie season in the Q, the NHL was not in the best of states. Financially, things were not looking good. Attendance was down leaguewide, television revenues were plummeting, and people were generally bored with the brand of hockey the NHL was producing. Ever since the leaguewide implementation of the trap, what was once a fast-paced, action-packed game became a slow, low-scoring defensive style of hockey that was not winning any new converts in the lucrative United States sports market. Both Mario Lemieux and Wayne Gretzky had complained about the clutch-and-grab style of hockey that was being practiced and had pointed directly at the game's state on the ice to the downfall of the sport. The NHL needed something or someone to save it. But saving had to wait another year, as the NHL lockout reared its ugly head and forced the cancellation of the 2004–05 season.

In an attempt to profit from the demise of the 2004–05 NHL season, two businessmen, Allan Howell and Nick Vaccaro, announced plans to start up an alternate league to feed the market's need for high-level hockey. The league would be called, of all things, the World Hockey Association (WHA) and would attempt to bring back the action-packed hockey that people wanted. The WHA, for those of you too young to remember, was a professional league that was started in 1972 and had teams from across North America (the Quebec Nordiques, the Winnipeg Jets, the Edmonton Oilers, and the New England Whalers all began in the WHA). The WHA back then attracted big-name hockey players like Bobby Hull and Gordie Howe and was the first place a 17-year-old Wayne Gretzky played professional hockey. The league ultimately failed, closing its doors in 1979 because it was no longer financially viable. Howell and Vaccaro, however, wanted to resurrect the WHA in hopes that people would turn to their brand of hockey instead of the NHL's. All they needed was a 17-year-old star to attract more players. In the summer of 2004, Sidney Crosby received a phone call offering him his first professional contract.

Nothing had been written in stone, and not one owner stepped forward to pay the $50,000 franchise fees, but that didn't stop Howell and Vaccaro, who offered Sidney $7.5 million for a three-year league commitment, with $2 million of that to be paid upfront. No one had any idea where the money was going to come from, but the fledgling WHA was willing to offer money it didn't have in order to lock in the young star. It wasn't even a question of money for Sidney Crosby. Along with a flat-out rejection of the offer, he simply wanted to play in the best hockey league in the world, against the best players in the world. Hoisting a Cup other than Stanley would not cut it. Besides, the amount of money he was offered paled in comparison to the endorsement deals alone that were sure to follow when he joined the NHL. But it was all a moot point, because the new league never even got off the ground.

All this talk of million-dollar contracts, NHL lockouts and new leagues was a little distracting, and Sidney was no doubt happy to get back out onto the ice for the start of his second season with the Oceanic. But this time around, things were a little different.

Chapter Five

Center Stage

Without a single NHL game to watch, Canadians every Saturday night wandered around their living rooms with blank stares etched on their faces, not knowing where to get their hockey fix. Canada was a nation in hockey withdrawal, and if it didn't get its fix, surely a revolution was not far behind. Luckily for the hockey hungry (author included), there was Sidney Crosby.

Lucky for us, not so lucky for Sidney. As he began his new season with the Rimouski Oceanic, hockey games that had never received any media attention in the past were plastered across newspaper headlines and made almost every evening news sports show. Everything Crosby did and said was passed over with a fine-tooth comb, making life a little more difficult than usual for him. Not that media attention was something he wasn't used to; Crosby probably had more microphones and television cameras shoved in his face than the biggest Hollywood star, and he was just 17 years old. With an attitude that said grin-and-bear-it, Crosby kept his game and his team in focus.

The Rimouski Oceanic's 2004–05 QMJHL regular season was indeed the one to watch for those seeking a hit of hockey. Although players around the league gave Crosby his fair share of whacks, face washes, elbows and more, he was protected like a precious jewel by his teammates. They knew that the key to their success was Sidney, and they were not about to let someone mess with their meal ticket. Try as hard as they might, they could not protect Sidney all the time, and during an October 1, 2004 game against the Halifax Mooseheads, someone got out of hand.

At that point in the season, Crosby was the team's number one scorer and helped the Oceanic off to a great 4–2 record. Games were high scoring, and Sidney's 18 assists were proof that things were generally going in the right direction. Both teams were poised to battle it out for league supremacy, and as this was their first meeting of the season, each wanted to set the tempo early.

The Halifax Moosehead player given the difficult task of guarding Sidney that night was

6-foot, 200-pound center Fred Cabana. It was
his job to shadow Sidney over every bump and
crack of ice surface to make sure he didn't get
the puck, and if he did, he was to be contained.
Sidney knew he was in for a rough ride that
night, and sure enough, every time Sidney
jumped on the ice, Cabana wasn't far behind.
But on one play in particular, Cabana went
a little too far in the completion of his on-ice
duties. Sidney was crossing the blue line into the
Halifax zone without the puck when Cabana
laid down a vicious knee-to-knee hit that sent
Crosby tumbling to the ice in obvious pain.
Through clenched teeth, Sidney let loose a litany
of harsh language that belied his normally boy-
ish charm. As Crosby was being carried off the
ice, teammate Patrice Coulombe without hesita-
tion skated directly after Cabana and delivered
a vicious check of his own that sent Cabana reel-
ing. Players from both sides rushed the frantic
scene, pushing and pulling, getting up in each
other faces and saying a few choice words their
grandmothers would be ashamed to hear. It was
a while before the referees got all the penalties
meted out and returned all gloves, helmets and
sticks to the offenders. Finally, the referees got
the players back into the game and got ready to
drop the puck. But before the puck even hit the
ice, Oceanic tough guy Alexandre Vachon

dropped his gloves and began raining down punches on the head of the Mooseheads' leading scorer Petr Vrana.

The crowd absolutely loved every second of the melee, but Sidney Crosby was not enjoying sitting in the dressing room with the doctors fussing over him. Like a true, gritty hockey player—the kind Don Cherry always likes to promote—Sidney had the trainer ice down his knee, and he got back in the game. He registered two assists in a losing cause, and when the adrenaline wore off after the game, his knee was in considerable pain. He tried to play a few more games, but the pain got worse and worse. After undergoing a complete exam, it was revealed that he only had deep bruising, but he would still miss several games.

For his harming of the league's most precious commodity, Cabana was given an eight-game suspension, and the league had harsh words for all players, saying that any reoccurrence of such violence would be dealt with swiftly and with an iron fist.

Crosby returned after a few games and easily fell back into his incredible goal-scoring streak. By the time the 2005 World Junior Championship rolled around, he had outpaced his previous year's production, scoring three points per game.

By late December, he was in peak form and ready for his second try at the 2005 World Junior Championship.

"I've learned a lot (since last year)," Crosby said. "I think I'm a better all-round player. I think I'm stronger and faster. I think after experiencing this tournament last year and finishing up in the Q and another half season this year, I have picked up things, like being more consistent defensively."

With the NHL lockout in full swing, the World Junior Championship was a chance to see some of the best young talent from around the world and to satisfy the need for quality hockey. The eyes of the world would be watching the arenas in the city of Grand Forks, North Dakota.

Hours before the start of Canada's first game against Slovakia, a caravan of rabid Canadian hockey fans crowded the Manitoba border crossings, all heading to the same place. Wearing their Team Canada jerseys and emphatically waving Canadian flags, they packed the arena to cheer on their young team. Not having any hockey to cheer about for months, they created a loud and enthusiastic atmosphere.

The Canadian media was omnipresent at the tournament. The sports networks of TSN and

Rogers Sportsnet descended on Grand Forks with an army of cameras and reporters ready to capture every angle of every play, savoring every moment of the mini-NHL-like atmosphere. And the player's name on everyone's lips was, of course, Sidney Crosby.

For all the fans traveling down to Grand Forks, and the millions at home watching, the World Junior tournament promised to be one of the most exciting in a long time. Canada's roster was one of the most dynamic in years, with guys like London Knights forward Corey Perry, Calgary Hitmens' Ryan Getzlaf, Sault Ste. Marie Greyhounds' Jeff Carter, Red Deer Rebels' Dion Phaneuf, Kitchner Rangers' Mike Richards—and with the Rimouski Oceanic's Sidney Crosby, Canada was almost guaranteed to go far, if not all the way to the finals. But it was not going to be an easy coronation. The Americans had a very solid team, but it was the Russians who showed early on in the tournament that they would be Canada's biggest threat. With the outstanding offensive talent of Alexander Ovechkin, Evgeni Malkin and Alexander Radulov, the Russians could easily surprise any team caught napping.

Canada handled the preliminary rounds with relative ease, defeating their first opponents, Slovakia, 7–3. Sidney and linemate Patrice Bergeron were the stars of the game, both scoring two goals apiece. The pairing of the two young players provided for some of the best highlights of the tournament. Normally a center, Crosby gladly switched over to right wing to accommodate Bergeron, who had played in the 2004 World Championship and had a full season of NHL experience.

In the second game against Sweden, the duo put on a show for the majority Canadian crowd as Sidney potted two goals, one of them from an impossible angle. Bergeron assisted on both of Crosby's goals and scored one of his own as Canada walked away with another easy 8–1 victory over the weary Swedes. Crosby's opponents tried to take him off his game any way they could. Hooks, holds and slashes did nothing to keep Sidney from attacking.

Speaking about one specific slash to his forearm during the game against Sweden, Sidney's response was simple enough. "You try not to get too unfocused when something like that happens. But when you're not near the puck and a guy does that, you want to be sure you bury a couple [goals]."

Canada then went on to destroy the Germans 9–0, with Sidney adding two more goals, and another win against the Finns 8–1 to finish off the round-robin portion of the tournament with a perfect record. That was six goals in four games for Crosby. But the round robin was just the beginning—if Canada lost a single game, then all those goals would not matter one bit. It was crunch time, and he knew the pressure was on. "What we've done is in the past. We know if we go out there and play the game, we are putting ourselves in a good spot to win," he said before the opening elimination round game against the Czech Republic.

Although the scoreboard suggested that Canada had made it by the Czech Republic with a close 3–1 victory, Canada actually only allowed the Czechs 11 shots in the entire game. It was an all-round defensive effort with Crosby pitching as well. Although he had less of an impact in the game, there was enough skilled scoring talent on the team to pick up for Crosby's lack in production. He still managed to pick up an assist on a goal by Patrice Bergeron, but sports pundits and coaches were not impressed by his presence in that game. In typical sports media fashion, Crosby was deemed a hero when he scored the six goals in the round-robin games, but after one mediocre game, a lot of airtime and newsprint was spent on pontificating about his performance or lack thereof. People still doubted Crosby and, as always, he kept proving them wrong.

The final was the classic match-up everyone was hoping for: Canada versus Russia, Crosby versus Ovechkin. When measuring the two young hockey phenoms side by side, it seemed Ovechkin had the upper hand. He was far more experienced with two international tournaments already under his belt, including the 2003 World Juniors in Halifax, where a 14-year-old Crosby watched from his spot on the bench as stick boy and where Ovechkin helped the Russians defeat the Canadians in the final. At 6 foot 2 and 210 pounds, Ovechkin also had Crosby beat in the size department, and so placing the match-up, on paper anyway, in Ovechkin's favor. After defeating the Americans in the semi-final game, and faced with an upcoming game against Canada, Ovechkin certainly did not seemed worried.

"Do you remember Halifax?" said Ovechkin, with a look of superiority on his face. "Everybody said that Team Canada would win the championship. We won. We proved that Russian hockey was better." Then he addressed all the talk about Crosby with equal calm. "I've never seen him play. I think he's a good player. But I don't play against Crosby. I play against Team Canada. Hockey is a team game."

It wasn't exactly a serious condemnation of Crosby's talent, but Ovechkin wasn't really even acknowledging him as a minor threat. Truth be told, no one expected Crosby to contain Ovechkin; it simply wasn't his role on the team. Crosby was a goal scorer, and that's what was expected of him. Containing Ovechkin was the job of the team's resident shutdown artist, Dion Phaneuf. He had more than enough size and toughness to match Ovechkin's stature and would look for every opportunity to line him up for the perfect check. But what happened at the midway point of the first period when Canada was up 2–0 surprised everyone in the building, and probably even Crosby himself.

Ovechkin led the Russian attack into the Canadian zone and, fearing a check from Phaneuf, he stopped at the blue line and cut across the middle. Big mistake. Coming in at full stride on the backcheck, Crosby laid a devastating hit on Ovechkin that sent the Russian superstar forward flying. Dazed and confused, Ovechkin skated back to the bench, and shortly afterwards, he pulled himself out of the game. Crosby had done something no one had thought possible: he took the Russians' best player out of the game and gave Canada the motivation it needed. Canada won the game by a final score of 6–1 and gave Sidney his first gold medal for Canada. As Canada's national anthem played on the loud speakers, Sidney was close to tears at having accomplished something he had always dreamed of as he sang the words to "O Canada."

After the game, Ovechkin showed up at the press conference with his arm in a sling and announced to journalists that Crosby had separated his shoulder on that play. Crosby later admitted that when he saw Ovechkin skating through the middle, he planned to lay the body on him. "Yeah, I knew it was him. And really, it was a situation that we knew to look for. We knew that nobody was challenging Dion [Phaneuf] in this tournament. No one beat him wide during the tournament and everybody stopped trying. And from watching him and from the scouting reports we knew that Ovechkin liked to pull up at the blue line and skate towards the middle."

Crosby wasn't chosen the MVP, he didn't lead in scoring, he didn't make the select tournament all-star squad, but he had the gold around his neck, and that was all that really mattered to him. "This is a dream come true," he said in the dressing room after all the official ceremonies were completed. "It's the best thing I've ever done, the best experience I've ever had. It's something you share with your teammates forever.... When you get older and look back, you'll be able to say you played with a lot of great hockey players."

This truly was the greatest assembly of World Juniors that Canada had ever seen; better than any of the teams that won five in a row; the best for a long time to come.

With his head still in a daze, Crosby packed his bags and began the journey back to Quebec to join his teammates in Rimouski. But when he got back to his room and finally sat down to unpack, Sidney noticed something was missing.

Chapter Six

The Case of the Lost Jersey, and the End of One Chapter

After returning from winning the gold medal at the World Junior Championships, Sidney Crosby wanted nothing more than to relive those days in his head. He had his memories, and he had the gold medal around his neck, but missing from his luggage was his number 9 Team Canada jersey. Crosby immediately called his parents and told them what had happened.

"There are no words to describe how disappointing and upsetting the whole thing is," said Sidney's mother Trina. "Its only value is sentimental, and that is for Sidney."

Word of the missing jersey soon got out, and it became the subject of a nationwide appeal. Troy Crosby addressed Sidney's disappointment in an interview with the *Globe and Mail*. "It's hard to explain what he's feeling. It's just a sick, sick feeling. No one can understand just how important that jersey is. It can't be replaced. Winning that gold medal was so special and the jersey is the one he wore while they did it. To go from such a high feeling to such a low feeling so fast is hard."

Theories began to surface as to how and why the jersey disappeared. Crosby was certain he placed the red jersey in his Rimouski Oceanic bag, and he had the bag with him before he got on the plane to head back to Quebec, so it must have disappeared going through the airport. It would not have been very difficult for an opportunistic baggage handler to figure out that it was Sidney Crosby's bag and that there might be something inside that would make a nice souvenir or fetch a handsome sum on the Internet.

Air Canada officials immediately responded by saying that there was no evidence that the sweater had gone missing in their care, but it was hard to think of another place it could have gotten lost, and it was not like it was the first time something valuable had been taken from someone's bags. Some people felt that the missing sweater didn't warrant enough attention to be featured on national media, but looking at it through the eyes of a 17-year-old kid who loved to play hockey and who truly and honestly dreamt his whole life of winning gold for his country, you had to have a pretty cold heart not to feel any sympathy for Crosby's plight. To Crosby, the jersey was just as important as the gold medal around his neck, and he definitely wanted it returned.

The gravity of the situation was compounded because the players' white sweaters were going to be auctioned off, with part of the proceeds going to the relief efforts for victims of the tsunami in South Asia that had occurred on Boxing Day in 2004. But because Sidney's jersey had gone missing, his white one was taken off the market and offered back to him as a replacement for the stolen one. Hockey Canada was willing to donate the over $20,000 in bids his sweater had received, but deep down Crosby wanted the jersey he wore when the gold medal was placed around his neck, and he refused to take back the white sweater. Sidney went back to work and continued to score goals for Rimouski, but in his heart he was still reeling over the loss of his jersey.

But a few days later, Crosby's face lit up when he got a call from the Montreal Police Department. They had found his red jersey. The police were not 100 percent sure the jersey was authentic, but when they told Sidney that it smelled bad, he felt sure that it was indeed his. "They said it smells pretty bad, so that's a good sign."

The jersey's adventure began in the baggage area at Montreal's Pierre Elliott Trudeau Airport when baggage handler Jacques Lamoureux noticed a Rimouski Oceanic bag was slightly unzipped, revealing a bright red sweater. He came up with the most tear-inducing story he could think of in hopes of distracting people from the fact that he had stolen the jersey.

"As a single parent, you can't always buy everything they (kids) ask for. I had just replaced all of her (his daughters) equipment. Pants, gloves, shin-pads. At this age, you have to have good equipment," said Lamoureux.

When he realized, so he said, that what he had done was wrong, Lamoureux immediately put the sweater in a bag and dropped it in a mailbox in Gatineau, Quebec. Two things more than likely occurred to him: first, that his daughter would never be able to show anyone the jersey, and second, that he could no longer sell the sweater now that the story had gone nationwide.

The next day on his regular rounds, postal worker Jean-Marc Saucier found the jersey, recognized whose it was and called Hockey Canada officials in Calgary. The following day, Sidney had his precious jersey back, and he smiled like a boy on Christmas morning. The would-be thief was fined $5000, suspended from his job and charged with theft.

With his jersey returned and his mind put to rest, Sidney got back on track and focused on the task of taking his Rimouski Oceanic to their ultimate goal, the Memorial Cup.

The 2004–05 season was something else! Sidney Crosby attracted attention wherever the Oceanic traveled. Fans eager to get a glimpse of the phenom even bought out many of the Oceanic's away games in order to see Crosby. On his last visit to Halifax to play the Mooseheads, Sidney's parents turned out with thousands of supporters, making the away game feel a lot more like a home game. Crosby scored two goals and helped with four assists as the Oceanic won the game 8–4. The score of the game really didn't matter, though; people had come out just to see him play hockey in the Maritimes one last time before heading off to the NHL. If they wanted to see him play again, they would have to travel to the closest NHL city, which was Montreal. The hometown boy had made good, and fans came to wish him well. Many hoped that the next time he returned, it would be with a Stanley Cup perhaps or with his Oceanic team in the QMJHL playoffs.

Despite missing some games of the World Junior's because of injury, Sidney bettered his previous season totals, scoring an incredible 66 goals and 102 assists in 62 regular-season games, which works out to an average of 2.7 points per game. The closest player in terms of points in the league was teammate Dany Roussin, who finished the season 54 points behind Crosby. With stats like that, Sidney again walked away with several awards, including the Canadian Hockey League's top player for the second consecutive year.

Awards aside, Sidney readied himself for the playoffs. All his personal accomplishments did not matter to him; it was the team's success that was important. The team finished off the regular season in style, with a record 28-game unbeaten streak and the odds-on favorites to win the Memorial Cup. It was Crosby's last year in the major junior leagues, and he wanted to finish with the QMJHL league championship and cap it off with a Cup win.

Rimouski's first opponents were the Lewiston Maineiacs, a team that finished 26 points behind the Oceanic, but they were a team determined to make their mark. Lewiston had their fair share of talent and gave the Oceanic a hard time at some moments, but Rimouski's high-powered offense, led by Crosby, was just too much for them. Lewiston was out of the playoff hunt, and Crosby and company moved on to their next opponents, the Chicoutimi Sagueneens.

Poor Chicoutimi had no idea what hit them. In the first two games alone they were outscored 18–2, and by the time they figured out a way to play Rimouski, they were out of the series in five games. Sidney was again the outstanding talent of the bunch, scoring 7 goals and 7 assists to lead his team in the finals of the QMJHL. The match-up could not have been better. It was Sidney Crosby's Rimouski Oceanic against the team from his hometown, the Halifax Mooseheads. The Mooseheads were probably the best team able to oust the Oceanic from the playoffs, but facing such a formidable offense with weapons like Crosby and his linemates Dany Roussin and Marc-Antoine Pouliot made their task difficult.

Game one was a relatively easy victory for Sidney and the Oceanic. Although they were out-shot, Rimouski took advantage of their opportunities and put the game well out of reach for the Mooseheads. Sidney helped out his team's cause by scoring a goal and two assists on the way to a strong 9–4 victory. Halifax needed to adjust their style in order to stop the Oceanic attack in game two, or the series would be finished.

In game two, the Mooseheads tried to keep the score level, but they could not keep up with Sidney and his mates. Down by two goals in the second period, the Mooseheads managed to come back to tie the game with two goals by Halifax's Petr Vrana, but it wasn't enough. The Oceanic pulled ahead and never looked back, winning the game by a final score of 7–5. In game three in Sidney's hometown of Halifax, the Mooseheads battled back from a 4–0 deficit but could not make up the difference, and the Oceanic took a 3–0 series lead. Game four was not much different. A huge crowd turned out to see Sidney Crosby, and although he was on the opposing team, every time he got the puck a chorus of cheers erupted from the crowd. Fans had turned out in droves to say goodbye to their native son. The game ended with a 4–3 Oceanic victory. Crosby finished the playoffs with 14 goals and 17 assists in just 13 games. Despite the hometown team's loss, the Halifax fans gave Sidney a standing ovation as he lifted the QMJHL President's Trophy high above his head.

"It's great to do it in front of my family and friends," Crosby said after the final game. "They've given me support my whole life and to do it here, the place where I grew up watching junior, is a great feeling. I think the fans back home would have liked to see us do it there but we got it and we're bringing it home."

Sidney and the Oceanic's next stop was the Memorial Cup tournament, Canada's premiere hockey tournament that every year decides the best major junior team in the country. But this year was unlike any other.

With the disappearance of the NHL, the media's attention was focused on the Memorial Cup alone. Add to that the star power of Sidney Crosby and the circus around the Cup, and the 2005 junior tournament seemed like a Stanley Cup final. For Crosby, this was exactly where he wanted to be, and he needed to be in perfect form to have any hopes of besting the mighty London Knights. Although the Ottawa 67's and the Kelowna Rockets made it to the tournament, they were completely outclassed by Rimouski and London, and they needed a miracle to make it into the finals. The tournament would finally put to rest which team was the best in Canada. It would also put to rest the comparison between Crosby and the Knights' scoring star Corey Perry. Neither player wanted anything to do with the comparisons, but this was the Memorial Cup, and sportscasters were dealing with a season without the NHL, so speculations and comparisons were bound to occur. Everyone was angry over the NHL and the lockout, and they came to the Memorial Cup to watch real hockey played by kids who played the game out of passion. The first game of the tournament ignited those passions as the London Knights played host to Crosby and the Oceanic.

After what seemed like an hour of opening ceremonies, Crosby finally took his spot at center ice and waited for the referee to drop the puck, like a lion ready to pounce on its prey. As soon as it hit the ice, Crosby took the puck and sped past the dazed Knights defensemen. Trailing not far behind was his trusty winger Marc-Antoine Pouliot, who accepted a beautiful backpass from Crosby but missed the short side of the Knights' net. Crosby was out to set the tone early. Although London got the first goal, their lead did not last long. Crosby tied the game with a power-play goal that bounced off a Knights' skate and into the net. Several shifts later, he assisted on two more Rimouski goals, giving his team a 3–1 cushion.

But the fast start seemed to have drained all the life out of the team, and in the second period the Knights began to crawl out of their hole. The game turned into a slash-filled, clutch-and-grab fest that created a steady rush of players to the penalty box, and the Knights paid particular attention to one player. Crosby had to deal with slashes, cheap shots and dirty gloves in the face, and at the end of the second with a 3–2 lead, frustration began to show in the Oceanic star as he screamed at the ref to do something about the obvious infractions. The flow of the game was brought down to a crawl, and that benefited the Knights more than anything, effectively removing Crosby as a threat. The third period saw the Oceanic lead evaporate, and the Knights finished them off with a 4–3 victory.

"They're everything that everyone said they were," said a frustrated Crosby after the game, surrounded by what seemed like 100 reporters. "Our goalie really helped us tonight and really kept us in the game. They had a lot of momentum coming through the second and the third and we just didn't get a lot going in those two periods."

After licking their wounds, Rimouski picked themselves up off the floor to play two games in two nights, against the Ottawa's 67's and the Kelowna Rockets. The games were tough and physically demanding on Crosby because both teams tried the same-old strategy of trying to physically intimidate Sidney, but again it failed. The 67's and the Rockets lost both games by a score of 4–3. Now it was time for the playoffs.

Because the Rimouski Oceanic lost one game against the Knights in the opening game of the tournament, they did not get the bye into the final rounds and were forced to play a semi-final match against the Ottawa 67's. Crosby was again the star of the match, scoring three goals and two assists, almost single-handedly defeating the 67's by a score of 7–4. The only game where he had anything else to prove would be the finals against the undefeated London Knights for the Memorial Cup Championship. It wasn't going to be easy. They had played them already and learned their lessons. Their key to the defeat of the Knights would be to sustain their attack for the full 60 minutes and be solid on defense against the Knights' equally potent offense. Rimouski was unfortunate to have played the 67's one night before the final, whereas the Knights had played their last game four days earlier. Things seemed to be piling up against the Oceanic, but if anyone could lift the team to victory, it most definitely was Sidney Crosby.

In front of their home crowd, the London Knights burst out onto the ice to thunderous applause. The Oceanic came out and were welcomed by a few jeers and polite clapping. More than anybody else on the ice, Crosby wanted to walk out of London's John Labatt Centre with the Memorial Trophy. The game promised to be a knockdown, dirty affair, but it could have only one winner.

Events did not go in Crosby's favor, however, for in the first few minutes of the game, the Knights seemed to have the trophy locked up. The Ontario Hockey League referee sent a Rimouski player to the box for a two-minute cross-checking penalty.[*] It was then that Rimouski enforcer Eric Neilson decided to punch Knights star forward Corey Perry in the face. Although it was just an intimidation tap, Perry went down as if Mike Tyson had hit him in the chin with a vicious right hook. Perry's theatrics got the call from the ref, and already in the opening minutes of the game the Oceanic were down two men. Crosby jumped on the ice to kill as much of the penalty as he could, but the moment he stepped off the ice to catch his breath, the Knights' Dan Fritsche scored, putting the home team up by one. The Rimouski bench all stared at their skates, seemingly realizing that the game was going to be an uphill battle.

---

[*]As pointed out by Gare Joyce in his book *Sidney Crosby: Taking the Game by Storm*. The Canadian Hockey league brings in officials from all three leagues for the Memorial Cup, giving the job of officiating the final to those who received the highest grades from the officiating supervisor. Therefore, a team can play in the national championship game with a ref who worked their games all year and knew the players very well.

Things were not any easier for the Oceanic's own star, as he was hounded throughout the game by Knights defenseman Marc Methot. Methot did everything he could to get Crosby off his game, and by the halfway point of the first period it appeared that he was doing a perfect job. Crosby was no threat during the first period and seemed more focused on the players than the puck. Knights defenseman Bryan Rodney put his team up by two before the end of the first period, and when the buzzer sounded for inter-mission, it looked as though the Oceanic had nothing left to give. They limped off the ice to the dressing room feeling dejected.

When they went back out on the ice for the second, nothing changed. Crosby tried to make some headway into the Knights' zone but kept getting locked up by their defense and couldn't get anything going. Maybe playing the game the day earlier had used up all their fuel, leaving nothing for the Knights. Maybe the pressure of the Memorial Cup was too much for the Oceanic. Maybe Crosby was having an off night. Or maybe the Knights were too good. By the third period, with the Knights up 3–0, the Oceanic just seemed to be playing out the clock. Through the noise of the crowd, the final buzzer sounded. Sidney looked up at the 4–0 score and was forced to watch while the Knights piled on top of each other, celebrating their victory. After the game Crosby was one of the last players to emerge from the safety of his dressing room to face the waiting reporters.

"The bottom line is we played a better hockey team," said Crosby.

Despite Oceanic losing in the final game, the Memorial Cup was a complete success for Crosby on a personal level. He finished the tournament with six goals and five assists in five games, leading all scorers. For his efforts he took home the Ed Chynoweth Trophy as top scorer and was given first team all-star status.

While Sidney continued to lament the Memorial Cup loss, the NHL and the Players' Association still could not come to an agreement, and it appeared that even the 2005–06 season was in jeopardy. The 2005 draft scheduled to take place in Ottawa was canceled, and the likelihood of Sidney being called up by a team was getting less and less. Asked what he would do if the NHL did not start up again in the fall, Sidney was as unsure of his future as the professionals trying to hammer out a contract deal. "I would not play in a replacement league. The NHL is the NHL for a reason. It's the best league in the world, and with replacement players would not be. The NHL with real NHL players is where I want to be."

Luckily, Sidney never had to make the tough decision on where to play, as the NHL and the Players' Association got their act together and announced in late summer that the 2005–06 season was a go, and that general managers could start crossing their fingers that they would get the number one pick.

Chapter Seven

The 2005 NHL Entry Draft

The lead-up to the 2005 NHL Entry Draft was nothing like the NHL had ever seen. After suffering for a year without the NHL during the 2004–05 lockout season, hockey fans everywhere were itching for the new season to begin. Making the season all the more exciting was wondering which team would win the Sidney Crosby draft lottery, otherwise known as the "Sidney Crosby Sweepstakes." Every team wanted him, but only one would be lucky enough to walk away with the number one overall selection.

The NHL Draft Guide for the class of 2005 lists player information and notes from scouts for each potential selection. Sidney Crosby's section in the guide was much longer than other players and listed a veritable cornucopia of qualities that any team would love to have on their side.

An exceptional skater with a smooth stride, tremendous balance and agility...he has great speed to the outside and can also split the defense carrying the puck or receiving passes for clear breakaways...very quick off the mark with tremendous acceleration...his vision is unparalleled...can feed wings from anywhere in the offensive zone both forehand and backhand and set them up for scoring chances...uses the hard crisp pass and puts it on the tape every time...can also use the soft flip pass effectively...his leg strength and stamina allows him to be the first on the puck and many times be the first guy back to help defense on transition.... Blessed with natural scoring instincts, he can score many ways and always seem to be in the clear to receive passes and turn them into scoring chances...needless to say he has great hockey sense; can play any position... can control the power play...good on faceoffs...very accurate wrist shot...his backhand is as good as the forehand...competes every shift, works hard but makes it look easy and plays with discipline...not adversely affected by physical play...takes many hits to make a play and will retaliate, which he has to do often because of the close checking and makes it look easy sometimes.

*Unselfish player who plays all game situa-
tions...logs a lot of ice time...at home or on
the road, does not matter to him; plays with
great poise...possesses great leadership qualities, desire and determination...will strip
opponents of the puck rather than punish
with the body.*

After a 310-day lockout that forced the cancel-
ation of the 2004–05 season, the return of the
NHL began with one of the most anticipated
drafts in recent history. Anticipated, because of
one 17-year-old from Cole Harbour, Nova Scotia—
someone all 30 teams would love to have on their
team. The draft that year was done a little differently, however. Normally, the number one spot
goes to the team that finished dead last in the
league, but because no one had a season to finish
last in, the number one selection went by lottery.
But it was a lottery with a catch. The lottery
was intentionally stacked. By way of selecting
balls out of a bingo-style drum, the teams
with the lowest number of points in the 2003–04
season got to put more balls in the drum than
teams that finished at the top, giving the weaker
clubs a better chance at the top pick. After several trial runs, the teams with the most balls
usually came out on top, but there were a few
occasions in the trial run where the "better"
teams won the Sidney Crosby Sweepstakes.

Before the actual draw, all the players, including the number one prospect, have to go through team interviews and physicals. Around 100 of the top prospects are invited to undergo a battery of tests, from push-ups, standing jumps, calisthenics, weight training, to the ever popular VO2 test on stationary bikes (designed to test the amount of oxygen consumed during rigorous activity, usually followed by the poor prospect of either passing out or vomiting from exhaustion). Next to come are the rounds of interviews with the interested teams, with no parents or agents allowed.

Crosby arrived for the fitness testing less out of wanting to prove himself than to take in the experience just like every other player. Any team would take him even if he smoked two packs of cigarettes a day—this was Sidney Crosby, and he did not need to prove himself physically able to play the game. Anyone who had witnessed his stunning run in the CHL playoffs knew that the 17-year-old was ready for NHL action. He was the type of player who everyone wanted to see and every coach wanted on his bench.

Every eye in the room focused on Crosby as he submitted himself for the general physical tests. He passed the battery of tests, but with average marks. It isn't the numbers that tell the story of a good hockey player; after all, any athlete can put up good numbers. Crosby had that intangible quality that scouts and general managers were looking for. The pre-draft festivities came to an end, and every team counted down the days until the names were plucked from the lottery and the lucky winner chosen. The lottery event takes place a week before the actual draft, and there was an air of excitement in the room as general managers and fans across the league kept their fingers crossed that they would win the Sidney Lottery.

It truly was a lottery in a sense. For some of the teams, attracting fans is a difficult task, and a player of Sidney's caliber, say, on a team like Atlanta, would definitely put more fans in the stands and increase revenues in other areas. Hearts were made lighter as well when Sidney announced before the draw that no matter what, he would play for any team that selected him and would not pull an Eric Lindros. (When Lindros was drafted, the Quebec Nordiques had the number one selection, but Lindros made it very clear that if they selected him, he would not show up at training and would request a trade.) There had been many highly touted hockey saviors in the past, but none turned out to be the genuine article. Sidney Crosby mania had finally arrived.

League commissioner Gary Bettman approached the microphone to begin announcing the draft's order of selection. From his home in Cole Harbour, Sidney watched the proceedings live on television, with a camera aimed directly at his face for instant analysis. Sidney, who had always been a Montreal Canadiens fan, did not try to hide his sentimental favorite choice, saying that it certainly would be nice to be a Hab, because his dad had been drafted by them. As the draft reached the 10th pick, the Canadiens had yet to be called. By the time the sixth pick rolled around, and the Canadiens still hadn't been called, Sidney got a little more excited, but then Bettman pulled out the fifth pick and named the Montreal Canadiens. A little disappointed, Sidney waited to hear where he would be playing hockey for the next couple of years. It was down to the Anaheim Ducks and the Pittsburgh Penguins. Sidney held his breath. Bettman opened the envelope to reveal the second pick; it was the Ducks. Sidney Crosby would become a Pittsburgh Penguin.

Other than Montreal, this seemed to be the perfect fit for Sidney. Mario Lemieux, a veteran in the twilight of his career, could teach the rookie a few lessons and know that he could leave the Penguins organization in good hands. It was the perfect marriage of talent and skill, and seeing them on the same line together had hockey fans everywhere just dying to witness the matchup. The start of the season could not come soon enough for some.

The selection of Sidney Crosby changed the fate of hockey in Pittsburgh. After winning the rights to Crosby, Lemieux, who had put the Penguins up for sale, removed them from the market and quickly went ahead on building a new arena. Crosby would transform hockey in Pittsburgh and bring it back to when Lemieux was the city's star. Asked if he would trade the first pick for anything, Lemieux shrugged it off with a hearty laugh. Pittsburgh Penguin jerseys with Sidney's name on them were already in production before the actual draft. Season tickets were being swept up in record numbers, and it looked like they would be sold out by September. It was boom time in steel town. Pittsburgh now just had to make the selection.

On a beautiful summer day at the end of July in downtown Ottawa, Sidney Crosby prepared himself for one of the biggest days in his life. He began the day with a vigorous workout at the hotel gym with fellow top prospect and good friend Jack Johnson. For Crosby, it was nice to remove himself from the insanity of trade day and chat with a friend. After getting himself ready, Crosby made his way down to the room where all the teams had gathered and waited to hear his name. After a few opening words of welcome, Gary Bettman finally gave the microphone over to Pittsburgh Penguin general manager Craig Patrick. "On behalf of Mario Lemieux and the entire ownership group, the Pittsburgh Penguins select, from Rimouski of the Quebec Junior League, Sidney Crosby."

And just like that, a new era in the NHL was born. Sidney Crosby walked up to the podium, shook hands with Penguin executives, put on the Penguins jersey and stood next to Mario Lemieux (the one with the biggest smile in the room).

"It's a special day for me. Sidney is a great talent," said Mario. "He loves the game of hockey, and he's going to be a great forward in this league. I'm looking forward to playing with him."

The pressure on Sidney was intense. Mario had put off the sale of the franchise in the hopes that the 17-year-old would bring new life back to the team and the city, and Sidney hadn't even played one game. In fact, he was not even on the team yet. Everyone, including the Penguins organization, felt that Sidney had made the team when he put on that jersey, but for Sidney, training camp was just another challenge. He humbly accepted that he would have to try as hard as everyone else to make the team. But he was already planning his strategy for when the season began.

"On the ice, I think I'd want to be someone who makes things happen offensively—definitely have to be a well-rounded player to play in the NHL today. That's something I've got to make sure I am," said Crosby. "Off the ice, just, you know, someone who is respected. Obviously I'm going to be young, I'm going to be a rookie. I'm going to try to learn as much as I can and just be someone who is open-minded and be a student." This is the attitude that every great hockey player has had: Wayne Gretzky had it; Mario Lemieux had it; Gordie Howe had it; Bobby Orr had it; Maurice Richard had it; and Sidney Crosby has it, too.

With a chance to review its on-ice product over the lockout, the NHL made some changes that benefited players like Crosby and put more excitement back into a game that had lost so many fans. The NHL was faced with a tough challenge. A few years before the lockout, fan dismay with the NHL had been growing. On-ice play had slowed down to a crawl compared to the early 1990s when scoring was high. For example, in the 1992–93 season, over 20 players in the NHL had accumulated 100 points or more, whereas in the 2002–03 season, only three players got over the 100-point mark. There was no steady flow to the game, and it was dominated by the defensively dull trap system. When the lockout occurred, many fans considered boycotting the league; there were countless angry letters to newspaper editorials calling out both the players and the league for their greed. Radio shows across Canada expressed disgust with what appeared to be a bunch of overpaid players and a collection of wealthy owners griping over money while real fans paid astronomical prices for tickets and had to watch a bad product on the ice. In Canada the lockout was huge news, but in the United States no one really even noticed the NHL was gone. Except for a few hardcore fans and cities like Detroit, Boston and New York, U.S. hockey fans just switched their attention to one of the other more popular sports. The NHL knew it was going to have to work to get back not only the fans but also the corporate support that was lost in the process. The Great One put the task into perspective:

"At the end of the day, everybody lost. We almost crippled our industry. It was very disappointing what happened. For everyone to say 'all right, let's forgive and forget, let's move forward,' that's all fine and good but it's a lot easier said than done. It's going to take a long time. It's going to take a lot of hard work. We disappointed a lot of people, and I don't mean the average fan. I'm talking about TV partnerships, corporate partnerships, the fan, the guy who goes to one or two games a year with his son. We've got a lot of work ahead of us. It's not going to all change and be nice overnight."

Truth be told, in Canada, the NHL did not have that hard a time bringing fans back onside. Hockey in Canada is an institution, and although there were some bitter feelings, Canadians were more than happy to have hockey back. In Pittsburgh, the arrival of Sidney Crosby could not have come at a better time. In the 2003–04 season, attendance at Mellon Arena was at an all-time low, with an average of just over 11,000 fans per game; in Montreal, the Habs had sold out the building with over 21,000 strong. But the league and the Penguins needed more than Sidney Crosby to save the NHL. Something was wrong with the game, and it needed fixing. To fix the problem, the league implemented a few new rule changes that were designed to speed up the game and increase scoring. After all, the trap system and clutch-and-grab hockey had kept superstars like Mario Lemieux and Wayne Gretzky from finishing off their careers with more points. The league did not want a player of Crosby's talent to be hampered by those same issues. Sidney needed to have the freedom to do what he did best if the league was going to survive.

One of the first changes was allowing the two-line pass, thereby creating some exciting Hail-Mary passes up the ice for breakaways. Goaltenders were also a prime target, as their equipment had ballooned to astronomical proportions. (For proof, look at Patrick Roy when he started with the Habs to when he finished with Colorado. There is no way he gained that much weight.) Goaltender pads got a good trimming, allowing an extra few inches for increased scoring. The most important change was the zero-tolerance attitude of the referees towards all the hooking, interference and holding that had previously plagued the NHL. The change that garnered the most interest with the fans, however, was the shootout to decide tie games during the regular season. With all these changes, Sidney Crosby was sure to get the breathing room he needed to become what the Penguins, the city of Pittsburgh and hockey fans hoped to witness.

"Obviously, this is a new level, but the pressure has always been there. I've always put a lot of pressure on myself to perform," said Crosby.

With Crosby signed on, Mario ready to be his line mate and a city behind them, the Penguins set about surrounding Crosby with the players who would best complement his skills. Crosby was soon joined by a host of new players: solid defensemen Sergei Gonchar and Lyle Odelein; forwards Ziggy Palffy, John Leclair and Mark Recchi; and goaltender Jocelyn Thibault.

After he signed on with Pittsburgh and even though he had not even played a single NHL game, Crosbymania was already sweeping the United States. Just a few days before his 18th birthday, Crosby got a call to appear on the *Tonight Show with Jay Leno*. It was Crosby's first major public appearance before an American audience who didn't even know he existed. Crosby appeared on stage in a dark striped suit with a collared shirt slightly open at the top, looking extremely relaxed and much more mature than his 17 years would suggest. Leno began the interview by asking Crosby how he got his start playing the game, which prompted Leno to show a photo of his mother's dryer dented by hundreds, if not thousands, of puck marks from when Crosby used it as target practice in his parents' basement.

"I hit it and then I'd hear upstairs, 'What was that?'" said Crosby. "I didn't say anything. But as you can tell, that took a bad beating. I wish you could see the top. There's not a button left on it. After a while she didn't care," he added. "But it took a bad beating."

The funny American host could not resist joking with Crosby, mimicking what Crosby would say to his mom now, "Mom, I'm making millions now. I've got you a new dryer." Leno further teased Sidney when he asked him if he could grow a playoff beard, to which he replied only a slight mustache.

After Crosby had answered a few more hockey-related questions, a dryer was brought out, and Leno asked Crosby if he could show the crowd how he practiced back home. Handed a stick and a few pucks, Crosby missed the center of the dryer the first two times, hitting the side of the machine. Then he missed on the left entirely. The last two pucks went in, and a slow-motion video replay was played on camera as Crosby's time on American television came to an end. The NHL had a new ambassador for the game in the United States, and Crosby's first appearance by all measures was a complete success.

Crosby was lucky enough to get a little time off after the insanity of the preceding few months and spent some quality time with his parents in Cole Harbour before moving in with his boss and linemate Mario Lemieux. It must have felt a little strange at first to be waking up in the morning and having breakfast every day with Mario Lemieux, but Sidney had just turned 18 at the beginning of August, and living with Mario for the first season was the perfect fit. He was surrounded by a friendly, family atmosphere, and he had the support of one of the greatest players in NHL history.

Chapter Eight

Training Camp and Beyond

On September 16, 2005, Sidney Crosby walked into Mellon Arena for his first professional training camp. Several months earlier he had been a 17-year-old prospect finishing up an unbelievable run to the Memorial Cup, and now he was thrust into the spotlight of the NHL. At times the media attention was a little overwhelming, but after dealing with intense media pressure from as young as seven years old, Sidney was more than able to take whatever people threw at him. But that didn't stop the young star from getting butterflies before he stepped out onto the ice.

"I was a little nervous. Obviously this is my first NHL camp, my first time skating with all those guys at once." As always, Crosby shrugged off the pressure and his emotions when he hit the ice. "Once I got on the ice and started playing I settled down pretty easily," said Crosby.

For the first time, the Penguins opened training camp at Mellon Arena to allow the public and the throngs of media to get the first look at the new kid. Media outlets, mostly Canadian, stationed their top sports reporters in Pittsburgh to cover every move Sidney made. He had finally achieved his goal, but now the expectations would be even higher.

Pittsburgh was overjoyed to have such a highly touted player on their team, but most people in the city had never even seen him touch a puck, let alone score a goal. The practice would be the city's first look at the young star, and everyone in the building had their eyes fixed on Crosby. After practice, Crosby did his best to please everyone who asked him for a piece of his time. On the ice he looked like a professional who had been playing for years; off the ice he became a humble, nice Canadian kid, happy to be doing what he loved. Although he was just a rookie and had practiced only once with the team, the veterans brought onto the team to complement Crosby made it sound as though he was complementing them.

"He's pretty smooth out there. It's fun to watch him," said veteran Mark Recchi. "His first couple of steps (are) incredible. He's making me feel young. I've got to try and keep up with him.

It will be good for Johnny (Leclair) and I to have a young guy that enthusiastic around."

After finishing off training camp, the Penguins moved to their farm team's building out in Wilkes-Barre, Pennsylvania, to play their first pre-season game against the Boston Bruins. In a building that can seat over 8000, only 5000 people showed up to see Sidney's first game as a Penguin. Not a great turnout when the Penguins' new star and its older legend both took the ice together for the first time, but Crosby rewarded those who did come out to see him with a strong effort.

In typical Crosby form, he worked hard all over the ice, making offensive runs and skating back to cover on defense. He fought along the boards, showing no sign of nerves when taking on big Bruin defenseman Hal Gill. Crosby nearly scored a goal, but the puck rolled off his stick before he had a chance to put it by the goaltender. Still, Mark Recchi was able to pick up the loose puck and give Sidney his first NHL assist.

"He's good on his skates, strong on his skates," gushed Mario Lemieux after the game. "He's amazing what he can do at 18. He just turned 18! In a couple of years he could be scary."

The pre-season passed, and Crosby was now ready (he made the roster of course). The day he had dreamed of for so long had finally arrived. Crosby played his first NHL game in New Jersey against the Devils on October 5, 2005. Walking the hallway between the dressing rooms, he skated out onto the ice for a light morning practice. As writer Shawna Richer describes, Crosby paused on the ice and looked up to the stands to where his parents and agent Pat Brisson were sitting, only to see them surrounded by a throng of reporters lined up to interview them on Sidney's big day. Sidney half chuckled to himself on seeing his parents undergoing the same thing he had to go through. All 30 teams were slated to play that day for the first time in history, but most eyes in the hockey world were focused on the Continental Airlines Arena in East Rutherford, New Jersey.

"It's going to be a good feeling, stepping out onto the ice. I am ready for it. I've been waiting a long time for this," said Crosby before the game.

The level of Crosbymania rose to such an extent that, on the day of the game, 150 members of the media where assigned passes to cover all aspects of that one game. Shawna Richer, in her book, *The Rookie*, detailed Crosby's day with precise detail. "On game day he woke up in the hotel....He showered and dressed in a dark suit and dress shoes and went down for breakfast shortly before 9:30 AM. He ate an omelette and yogurt, drank orange juice and bottled water, and talked quietly with some of his teammates." When Wayne Gretzky, Mario Lemieux and Eric Lindros came into the league, no one seemed to have this much information on their daily movements and habits.

And then came game time. Crosby skated around during the pre-game warm-up, not talking to any teammates but simply thinking to himself. He was nervous but excited to get things underway. Waiting in the hallway for the teams to be announced, he bounced back and forth on his skates, and when the announcer called out the Penguins, he stepped out onto the ice to a chorus of boos. This was the NHL, and fans were not going to be easy on him. Crosby did not start, but 32 seconds into the period he got the tap on the shoulder from head coach Ed Olczyk and jumped over the boards straight into the action. Showing his obvious flare for the dramatic, Crosby made a nice interception in the neutral zone and swooped down on goaltender Martin Brodeur. The veteran easily brushed the attempt off to the side. Crosby didn't score, but he made his presence known. In the third period, he got another chance in behind Brodeur's net and made a nice crisp pass to Mark Recchi's stick to give the Penguins their only goal of the game in a 5–1 opening-night loss. Despite losing, after the game Sidney asked for Martin Brodeur's stick to keep as a reminder of his first game and his first scoring chance.

Three days after his first NHL game, Sidney was back in Pittsburgh to open the season at Mellon Arena against the Boston Bruins. The sellout crowd of 17,132 was eager to get their first glimpse of Crosby and to see what all the hype was about. Sidney's parents were once again on hand to witness this pivotal moment in their son's career. They didn't have to wait long for their son to prove to the sellout crowd why he had been the topic of so much discussion.

At the beginning of the second period, with Pittsburgh up 5–4 on the Bruins, the Pens were on a power play, and Sidney was sent out to do his thing. Hovering around the net, the puck hopped onto Crosby's stick, and he smacked it towards Bruins goaltender Hannu Toivonen. Both Mark Recchi and Ziggy Palffy tried to smack the puck into the net, but it bounced onto Crosby's stick. Crosby was waiting at the side of the net, and he simply pushed the puck past the sprawled out Bruins goaltender. It wasn't the flashy type of goal that Crosby was used to scoring, but it was his first, and he was really happy about it. After scoring, he slammed his back into the boards and screamed as his teammates surrounded him and gave the congratulatory pats on the helmet. Up in the stands, Crosby's parents shed tears of joy at the realization of their son's hope and dreams.

That wasn't the end of his night, though. Crosby set up Brooks Orpik with a beautiful pass that had eyes of its own, and he also set up Ric Jackman with another amazing pass. However, it was not all good news, as the Bruins came back to tie the game and win it with a final score of 7–6 in overtime.

For his efforts in a losing cause, Crosby was named the game's first star and skated out to salute the crowd. The fans seemed to forget that the Penguins lost the game and cheered Crosby like a conquering hero. In the dressing room later, he posed for pictures with the tape-wrapped puck, "First NHL goal, October 8, 2005" written in bold letters.

Crosby was not happy about losing the game, but he did not remain morose for too long and gushed when asked about scoring his first goal. "I looked forward to it for a long time. It feels awesome. I was happy. It's something you dream of, scoring in the NHL, and you only do it for the first time once. It was big. There's a lot of emotion. The fans were great. It was so loud. I never expected to hear them chanting my name. You never expect that."

The next dream for Crosby was to win a game with the Penguins. Two days after getting his first NHL goal, Crosby and the Penguins traveled to Buffalo to play the Sabres. Crosby added another assist to his totals, but the Pens still lost the game in overtime. Out of 30 teams in the NHL, they were the only ones without a win. They lost the next game against the Philadelphia Flyers, then another loss to the defending Stanley Cup champion Tampa Bay Lightning, then another to the New Jersey Devils. They rolled into Boston's TD Banknorth Garden hoping to grab a win for their eighth game of the season.

Things were not going well in the Pens dressing room, and it was beginning to show on the ice. Before the game against the Bruins, Crosby dressed quietly in his corner and thought over how far he had come and how much he wanted that one victory. But his frustration grew even more as the Bruins jumped out to a 5–1 lead by the third period. After finishing one shift, in an unusual moment of anger and frustration, Crosby took his stick and smashed it on the boards, sending pieces flying in all directions.

The Pens ended up losing the game 6–3 despite Crosby's two assists and consistent effort each shift. He was making the odd mistake, but the team wasn't playing as a unit, and that resulted in losses.

"The first few games, I was just happy to be in the NHL and I didn't think much about losing because I was just happy to be here. But now that I'm here and working hard and we haven't got a win yet, it's tough. Winning is fun. Losing isn't. This hasn't been a fun time lately. That's for sure. We dig ourselves in a hole and can't deal with it," said Crosby after losing his eighth straight NHL game.

Yet, the worst was not over. Two nights after their eighth loss in a row, the Pens lost yet again in overtime to the Florida Panthers. After the game, Lemieux did not talk to reporters and stayed away from his teammates. It was the Penguins' worst start to the year in team history, and it looked as though they would never get out of their slump. After nine losses in a row, head coach Ed Olczyk began to worry about keeping his job and desperately searched for a way to pull his team out of their nosedive. For the next game against the Atlanta Thrashers, he juggled the lines, most notably pairing Lemieux with Crosby and Recchi. It was his hope that the line change would shake the players out of their funk and that playing the struggling Thrashers, who themselves had lost six of their seven games, would finally propel them to a win.

Olczyk's hopes were utterly crushed when Atlanta thrashed the Penguins with four straight goals in the first 10 minutes of the game. Desperate, Olczyk called a timeout and gathered his players around the bench. The Penguins had hit rock bottom, and the only way out was up. Whatever he said on the bench seemed to light a fire under the team, as the Penguins came back with a flurry of goals and won the game 7–5. Crosby got two assists in the game. The team was so happy when the final whistle sounded it was as if they had won the Stanley Cup.

For Crosby, his first month in the NHL ended with his team winning one in 10 games, but the rookie still managed to record two goals and 12 assists, earning him the league's rookie of the month honors, just beating out Alexander Ovechkin who had 8 goals and 5 assists.

After the first 10 horrible games, things started to gel for the Penguins. The first line of Crosby, Lemieux and Recchi was playing well and seemed to be in sync on the ice. Next to Crosby, Lemieux finally looked like he was enjoying what many knew would be his last season in the league.

The Penguins won a few more games and lost a few, but it mattered less, now that they felt they were coming together as a team. Then came the game that Crosby had been waiting for all his life. On November 10, 2005, the Montreal Canadiens rolled into Pittsburgh to play the Pens. This was the team that had drafted his father, and the team that he grew up watching. The moment was a special one for Crosby. The Habs were the most familiar team to him, in the most familiar building, and standing to listen to the national anthems was something he would never forget. "It's going to be special. It's the team I grew up watching. It's pretty cool." He was a kid again.

With the game finally underway, Crosby helped his team to an early lead when he got credit for a goal that bounced off the skate of Montreal Canadiens defenseman Francis Bouillon to give the Pens a 1–0 lead. Lemieux later added to the Pens' lead when he chipped a goal past Habs goaltender Jose Theodore to make it 2–0. But the Penguins could not hold the Canadiens attack off for long, and when the third period ended, the score was tied 2–2, and the game was headed for overtime. When that didn't solve anything, it was time for the shootout.

Michael Ryder, Alex Kovalev and Alexander Perezhogin all missed for the Canadiens, and

Lemieux and Recchi also missed on their chances. It came down to Sidney Crosby. If he scored, the game was over; if he missed, the shootout would continue and give the Canadiens a chance to steal the win. Sensing the weight of the moment, the crowd at Mellon Arena fell strangely silent as Crosby skated up to the puck. In a few strides he bore down on the Canadiens goaltender, and with a sneaky fake kick of the leg, forced Theodore to commit. Crosby then put a hard backhand past the sprawled out goaltender into the roof of the net that sent the water bottle flying in the air. The crowd erupted when the red light went on, and Crosby was immediately swarmed by his teammates. Troy Crosby was sitting in the stands and probably jumped higher than anyone else when his son scored the winner.

Crosby was glowing after the game. "To do it in this type of game, with all the emotion and against the Canadiens, it's awesome. It was my favourite team growing up. Just to do it at home, it's a pretty amazing feeling. The fans stayed with us. They gave us the energy we needed."

The games up to that time had been tough for Crosby, but it was nothing compared to the battle he faced when the Penguins met their state rivals, the Philadelphia Flyers. The history of bad

blood between the two teams has been well doc-
umented over the years, and despite the new,
tougher rules of the NHL, the feud continued.

On November 16, 2005, the Penguins walked
into the hostile Wachovia Center in Philadelphia
to play their first game of the season against the
Flyers. Getting the call in the Pittsburgh nets for
the game was the young Marc-Andre Fleury,
who had been called up from the farm team
because of an injury to veteran goaltender Jocelyn Thibault. Lemieux was also out of the game
with the flu. It wasn't going to be an easy night
for Crosby.

The game started off normally enough, and
the first period passed without a goal or incident.
But with about six minutes left in the second
period, 6 foot 5, 230-pound Flyer defenseman
Derian Hatcher and Crosby got tangled in the
corner fighting for the puck. Not used to having
someone of Crosby's size battle so hard for the
puck, Hatcher was obviously frustrated and
decided to take it out on Crosby's face with his
stick. The attack sent Crosby onto the ice, crash-
ing on top of Hatcher's stick. He dragged Crosby
on the ice for a few moments while the young
Penguin kept his head down, and blood dripped
all over the ice. Crosby pulled himself up and
found that bits of his teeth had broken off.

Hatcher skated away like nothing had happened. The referees didn't see it, despite the young star's bloody face and chipped teeth.

Hatcher got away with the assault, while Crosby had to leave the ice to get four stitches to repair the gash in his mouth. Five minutes later, he returned to the ice, and there was Hatcher on the ice waiting for him. Just before the faceoff, Hatcher used his stick again on Crosby, this time hitting him in the throat, and again the referees saw nothing. Crosby was clearly frustrated and let the refs know just how much in some colorful language. For his uncharacteristic use of foul language, Crosby was given a two-minute unsportsmanlike penalty. Clearly angered, Crosby decided the best revenge was not physical but up on the scoreboard.

Had Hatcher seen Crosby playing in the Quebec Major Juniors, he would have known that Crosby had dealt with thugs like Hatcher before, and that every time they had tried to get him off his game he responded not with fists but with goals. Late in the third period Crosby assisted on a beautiful tic-tac-toe play with his linemates, setting up Ryan Malone for the opening goal. Not satisfied with the one goal, Crosby came back out less than one minute after the first goal and blasted a puck through traffic past Flyers goaltender Antero Niittymaki for the 2–0 lead. Crosby pumped his fist in the air and screamed at the top of his lungs. But the air in his lungs was quickly taken out as the Flyers defender Joni Pitkanen scored two quick goals to tie the game. With just seconds remaining to play, the Penguins were headed into overtime, a place they had not fared well that season. Crosby was on the ice like a man possessed, ready to seek his revenge on Hatcher the only way he knew how, by scoring.

Ryan Malone caught Crosby with a crisp pass as he hopped off the bench. Crosby took it and, finding himself all alone, bore down on the Flyers goaltender. Niittymaki tried to come out to cut down the angle, but Crosby had too much speed coming into the zone and forced the goaltender into the net. It was while Niittymaki was backing up that Crosby spotted an opening on the goalie's stick side and slapped the puck in for the game-winning goal. The crowd booed, but as the great Scotty Bowman once said, "Every boo on the road is a cheer," and Crosby was loving every minute.

While Crosby was becoming the number one attraction on the team, the former star of the Penguins began to slow down. Mario Lemieux's shifts were getting shorter and shorter, and he missed a few games because of a mysterious illness classified as the "flu." But Lemieux was suffering from more than the flu. About halfway through the season, Mario just wasn't magnificent any longer. Then came the shocking news why he had been slowing down. Very soon Sidney would be handed the reins of the Penguins and be given the chance to write his own destiny.

Chapter Nine

The New Era

On December 7, 2005, while the Penguins were in the middle of a vigorous practice, several players noticed that Mario Lemieux looked a little pale and exhausted. Worried about his health, Lemieux checked himself into the hospital and found out that he was suffering from an irregular heartbeat, which untreated was a life-threatening condition. And as news of yet another health setback for Lemieux hit the media, it became clear to his teammates that their captain would not be part of the team much longer. The stress of playing, the stress of securing a new building and the stress of having to deal with the distinct possibility of losing the franchise all seemed to weigh heavily on Lemieux's heart.

Despite small victories, the Penguins still were not winning hockey games, and by mid-December they shared the bottom of the league

with the St. Louis Blues. It was clear that something had to change with the Penguins. Crosby
had never been in such a situation and was getting increasingly frustrated. His informal chats
with the media after the games were getting
shorter and shorter, and on a few occasions he
didn't make himself available. On December 14,
the Penguins headed west to play the lowly
St. Louis Blues, a game they hoped to win. But
the Penguins did not play like they wanted to
win, and Crosby at times looked like he was trying to do everything on the ice just to win. Frustration was evident on everyone's face. It also
proved to be head coach Ed Olcyzk's last game
with the Pens. The next day, it was announced
that former Montreal Canadiens head coach
Michel Therrien would take over the difficult job
of turning around a group of players who had all
but given up on their season. For Therrien, the
challenge of getting the franchise back in order
was exactly the type of job he was looking for,
and having Crosby to coach was an added
bonus.

"He's got so much skill and speed, for a coach
it's fun to have an opportunity to work with
that. I want to give him a chance to expose his
talents. He's going to be able to do a lot of good
things out there. I'm going to give him a lot of
opportunity. He does such amazing things on

the ice. I was impressed when I saw him in training camp, but I never thought he'd be this good," said Therrien.

Therrien's first major move as head coach was to name Crosby the alternate captain. There were several critics of the move—since he was the youngest ever to have the honor of wearing the "C" on his jersey—most notably the CBC *Hockey Night in Canada* vocal critic Don Cherry. Crosby took the high road and chose to leave the matters of the team in the dressing room. He took the appointment as a sign of honor. With Mario Lemieux out indefinitely, the Pittsburgh Penguins were now basically Crosby's team.

Going into the holidays, Sidney got a nice break from the hockey world and went home to Cole Harbour to spend Christmas with his family. It was a welcome vacation for the young star, who simply wanted to feel normal again. But when he returned to play for the start of the new year, Sidney confirmed that he was anything but normal when he made his first scheduled visit to play in Canada with back-to-back games in Toronto and Montreal. If he thought the attention in the U.S. was overpowering, he was in for a surprise.

Being in Toronto and witnessing the crush of media around him was a little overwhelming for

Crosby, but that attention was nothing compared to what La Belle Province had in store. Quebeckers had a special place in their hearts for Sidney Crosby. He had played in the Quebec Major Junior leagues and had made many friends and fans on his tours throughout the province while playing for Rimouski. Many of those same people made the trip to Montreal that cold January day to say hi and to cheer on their favorite player. But Crosby had also endeared himself to the Quebec people by taking the time to learn French during his time with the Rimouski Oceanic. Just as able to conduct interviews in French as in English, he managed to reach out to a whole new fan base that Gretzky, and especially Lindros, never could. Praise in the French media was often hard to come by if you were not a hometown boy, but Crosby, who was born in Nova Scotia and grew up a "bloke," was treated with the same respect and reverence that was normally accorded to Mario Lemieux.

The last time Crosby had been at the Bell Centre was when he was 12 years old and his dad took him to see a playoff game between the Canadiens and the Sabres. It was like a dream come true for the lifelong Habs fan, and now that he was on the other side of the dream, he relished every moment.

"It's special, not only for my dad, but for my whole family. We pretty much all grew up Montreal fans, but with him being drafted by them, seeing me playing in this building against a team that drafted him, I'm sure it's a little more special," said Crosby in a pre-game press conference.

Just before the puck was dropped and Crosby's name was announced for the Penguins starting lineup, the Bell Centre erupted into a symphony of cheers and applause. It was an unusual welcome for a visiting player, especially for the player who had scored the shootout winner against the home team a few months earlier. But Montreal fans appreciated quality hockey, and Sidney provided some of the best quality out there.

Crosby opened up the scoring when he beat Jose Theodore with a wrist shot from the top of the circle, to the delight of the sprinkling of Penguins fans. It was Crosby's 20th goal of the season. The Penguins used the momentum from Crosby's goal to put them ahead in the game 3–0, but by the end of the second period the Canadiens surged back with four unanswered goals to make it 4–3. The Pens added a late second-period goal to tie it up, and they headed into their dressing room not knowing what to expect in the fast-paced, high-action game. The Bell Centre was alive with excitement as the third period began.

Of course, it was Sidney Crosby who came through with the clutch goal at the midway point of the third period and gave the Pens all they needed to walk away with a 6–4 victory. Although the Canadiens lost the game, fans were treated to a wonderful exhibition of skill and high scoring.

Crosby was starting to like playing his boyhood team. If there was any doubt as to his popularity in La Belle Province, that was put aside when the French newspapers devoted almost 20 pages to Crosby and the Penguins. If the Canadiens didn't win the Cup, it was guaranteed that many Quebec residents would be cheering for Sid the Kid.

The Penguins had a few days between games and decided to stay in Montreal to practice before leaving for their next destination. Somehow, word got out that the team was at the Verdun Auditorium, and hundreds if not thousands of fans descended on the small arena to get a look at Sidney. When practice was over and Sidney made his way to the team bus, he was mobbed like a teenage pop star. Girls called out his name, middle-age men embarrassed themselves in an effort to get his autograph, and Crosby was caught in the middle trying to be as polite as possible while trying to hurry to the team bus. His teammates were already on the bus and rolled their eyes at the commotion caused by Sidney. It was a little overwhelming, but Crosby was certainly flattered.

Despite the win over the Habs, things in the Penguins organization were not getting better. The team was still putting up a losing record, and on January 23, 2006, Mario Lemieux called a press conference to announce his retirement once and for all. His heart had grown weary and could not take the stress of NHL hockey anymore; the Magnificent One was no more. He'd scored his last goal, fittingly enough, against the Montreal Canadiens. Pittsburgh was now Sidney Crosby's team.

As the season began to wind down, the Penguins still hadn't turned their fortunes around, but the team seemed happy that they did not have the pressure of trying to make the playoffs. For Crosby it was a bitter disappointment, because all his life he was so used to winning. But his season was not without its rewards. He finished the season with an incredible 102 points—the youngest player ever to do so—and was sixth in the scoring race. He was bested by fellow rookie Alexander Ovechkin for the Rookie of the Year Award but won the hearts of many new fans as one of the best players to watch in the future. He also received the distinction of becoming the first rookie in NHL history to score 100 points and accumulate 100 penalty minutes in the regular season, and he broke Mario Lemieux's rookie scoring mark of 100, with 102 points.

As for the Penguins, their fortunes changed over the summer. The Pens brought in a new general manager to replace Craig Patrick. Ray Shero was a shrewd businessman who knew how to get things done and recognized good talent when he saw it. The Penguins were also able to work out their issues with the Russian Super League and got star prospect Evgeni Malkin onto the team.

With a good group of moldable young players, the Penguins completely turned their luck around in the 2006–07 NHL season. They began to gel as a team, and the goaltending of Marc-Andre Fleury was proving solid. Crosby turned up his game (if possible) and scored his first hat trick on October 28, 2006, against the Philadelphia Flyers (Hatcher wasn't laughing now). Crosby continued to add to his list of achievements when he recorded his first six-point game in December (one goal, five assists) and led the NHL in scoring for the rest of the season. After the last game of the season, he had 120 points and led the league in scoring with 36 goals and 84 assists in 79 games. At only 19 years of age, Crosby was the youngest player in NHL history to win the Art Ross Trophy, and the youngest scoring champ in any major North American professional sport.

Finishing the season with a 47–24 record, the Penguins assured themselves a spot in the playoffs, and Crosby got his first taste of the post-season when the Pens met up against the Ottawa Senators in the first round. Like the high-scoring, high-flying Edmonton Oilers of the early 1980s, incredible offensive talent and a stellar regular season does not always translate into playoff success (it took Wayne Gretzky's Oilers several seasons before winning the Stanley Cup), and the Penguins had the same lesson taught to them by the Senators. Crosby and his young squad tried as best they could, but the Senators top line of Daniel Alfredsson, Jason Spezza and Dany Heatley could not be stopped. The Penguins were defeated in five games, and once again Crosby had to watch the Stanley Cup finals from home.

Despite the early exit from the playoffs, the Pittsburgh Penguins organization was convinced of Crosby's leadership skills. On May 31, 2007, he was offered the job of team captain. It was the perfect fit for a young, up-and-coming club to name their promising star to team captain. No one liked winning more than Sidney Crosby, and that sort of attitude was infectious. With a new captain and a new direction, the possibility of a Cup in Pittsburgh looked more promising by the day.

In June 2006, Crosby traveled to the NHL award ceremony to add two other trophies to his increasing collection: the Hart Memorial Trophy, given to the player adjudged most valuable to his team; and the Lester B. Pearson Award, given to the most outstanding player during the regular season as voted by the NHL Players' Association. Crosby became the youngest player ever to win the Lester B. Pearson Award and the second youngest to win the Hart Trophy, behind Wayne Gretzky. After Crosby took home his silverware, the Penguins wanted to lock in their star to a long-term contract, and after some negotiation, Crosby signed with the Penguins until the 2012–13 season for $43.5 million, which works out to exactly $8.7 million per season. (He managed to convince the Penguins to pay him the same amount as the number on the back of his jersey. Superstitious?)

Crosby easily could have signed for more money, but he wanted to be a part of a winning team, and if all the Penguins' money was locked up in one player, then the team would surely fail. By taking less, as it were, Crosby showed how committed he was to Pittsburgh and to making the team a winner again.

"Individual honors and scoring championships are great, but my No. 1 goal is to win the Stanley Cup. I'd love to be a part of bringing the Cup back here to Pittsburgh," he said.

The 2007–08 season started off well for Crosby and the Penguins. By mid-December, he added another milestone to his career with an unlikely Gordie Howe Hat Trick (which refers to Howe's ability to score a goal and an assist and to get into a fight all in the same game). In a game on December 20, 2007, against the Boston Bruins, Sidney assisted on a goal 55 seconds into the first period. Later in the first period, he scored his only goal of the game to give the Penguins a 2–0 lead. The Bruins knew that Crosby had to be stopped or they would most likely lose the game, and they assigned Andrew Ference to shadow his every move. After two periods of constant annoyance, when Crosby and Ference went into the corner after the puck, the two came together and dropped their gloves. It was a pretty even fight, with Crosby having a slight height and weight advantage. Although Ference took Crosby down to the ice, Ference got the worst of it, taking several right hands to the forehead and walking away with a bloody face. Afterwards, Crosby responded to the pack of reporters who gathered around him in the dressing room.

"It was one of those weird things that happen," Crosby said. "You don't really plan it, and that's all I'm going to make out of it. I did all right....It's not something I do too often."

With his season rolling along well and on pace for another 100-point season, Sidney was taken out of the lineup when he suffered a high ankle sprain in a game against the Tampa Bay Lightning in January. The injury took him out of the lineup for 21 games, but after returning he decided that he was not quite ready to come back to play and took himself out of the lineup for seven more games so that he could heal properly. He returned on March 27, 2008, to help the Penguins beat up on the New York Islanders and help the team finish their season and head into the playoffs as the second-best team in the Eastern Conference. In 53 games that season, Crosby scored 24 goals and 48 assists for 72 points.

Chapter Ten

The Playoffs

The Penguins marched into the playoffs with the third best record in the league and with a load of confidence after a brilliant end to the season. Sidney Crosby was firing on all cylinders and the team was following right behind their young captain. There would be a few obstacles on the path to the Stanley Cup finals, but the Penguins were confident and after having come out of the first round of the playoffs with a 4-0 series sweep of the Ottawa Senators, Crosby and the Penguins set their eyes firmly on the ultimate prize. Next up the New York Rangers.

Seventeen years earlier, a young, talented kid with amazing skills and little experience entered the playoffs wearing the number 68 on the back of his jersey and a black and gold penguin emblazoned on the front. New York Ranger Jaromir Jagr's entrance into the world of the NHL all those years ago resembles almost exactly the rise of Sidney Crosby. Both Jagr and Crosby entered the league with huge expectations (though Crosby had more weight on his shoulders), both started with the Pittsburgh Penguins and, of course, both of them profited from being under the wing of the Magnificent One, Mario Lemieux. The two Lemieux prodigies were without their teacher for their first meeting in the second round of the 2008 playoffs.

"I was pretty young when he was here," Crosby said of Jagr, the second leading scorer in Penguins history next to Lemieux. "I remember those two together and I remember how much they dominated and how he (Jagr) was always on the highlight reel with goals."

Mutual feelings of respect aside, a job had to be done, and the fans were ready for the evening's entertainment. The Rangers brought to the series their veterans and years of regular-season and playoff experience, while the Penguins brought their youthful enthusiasm and amazing talent. The series promised to be one of the young Pittsburgh captain's most difficult to date, and he would have to rally his equally young team to defeat the veteran players. Crosby knew never to underestimate players like Brendan Shanahan who was earning his scars in the playoffs, while young Penguin Evgeni Malkin was learning how to make friends on the playground in Russian grade school. It had all the makings of an exciting series.

"This is going to be a great seven-game series," said Penguins defenseman Ryan Whitney.

The challenge ahead was not lost on the Rangers Scott Gomez. "It's going to be a big challenge. You can't take a break with this offense....The guy (Crosby) is the best in the world," Gomez said. "He is great for our league. Everyone talks about LeBron James (NBA), and we've got someone like that in our league."

Ranger Jaromir Jagr was less diplomatic about facing off against the young Crosby and Malkin tandem. "With all due respect for Crosby and Malkin, I don't think they are Mario Lemieux," Jagr said. "I'm saying all the respect to them, but it's because the game has changed....The gap between Mario and the rest of the guys when I was in Pittsburgh was so huge....I don't think these kids are able to do it. Maybe I'm wrong."

Jagr would soon find out.

In the first two periods of game one, the Rangers schooled the young Penguins on adjusting to playoff pressure and took a 3–0 lead by the early stages of the second period, effectively silencing the normally raucous Mellon Arena and the

Penguins faithful flock. Fortunately for the fans, Jarkko Ruutu scored at the halfway point in the second. The goal seemed to ignite a fire under the Penguin bench, and Crosby's line immediately jumped out on the ice. Just seconds after the face-off at center ice, Crosby took control of the puck in the Rangers' zone, got the puck over to linemate Pascal Dupuis and in the blink of an eye the Penguins were within one goal of tying up the game.

In between the second and third periods, the Rangers dressing room was tense with emotion as the players could sense a definite shift in the game, but this was why the Rangers had signed veteran players like Brendan Shanahan and uber-pest Sean Avery to help them get over adversity in the playoffs. The Rangers knew Crosby was the glue that held his team together, and throughout the night he was the object of the Rangers' attention. However, this strategy was doomed to fail because, although taking out the highly talented Sidney Crosby is a good strategy, the Penguins possess a myriad of talented players who can burn any team at any moment, and at the 4:40 mark of the third period, Marian Hossa put the puck behind goaltender Henrik Lundqvist on a shot that deflected off Ranger Scott Gomez. The Mellon Arena announcer had barely begun to say Hossa's name when Malkin,

Ryan Malone and Petr Sykora broke in on two hapless defensemen and put the Penguins ahead for the first time.

The goal might have sent the Rangers packing their bags, but Jaromir Jagr shot a pass out from behind the Penguin net and found Scott Gomez for the one-timer to bring the game back to even, at four all. But luck was on the Penguins side as the Rangers Martin Straka took an interference penalty with only 3:20 remaining in the game. In the dying moments of the game, Crosby, who had been relatively quiet on the score sheet, turned on the afterburners.

Taking a pass from Ryan Whitney, Crosby crossed into the enemy zone and unleashed a rare canon of a slapshot that clipped Evgeni Malkin's leg and hit the back of the net for the game-winning goal. Malkin was given credit, but all he did after the game was talk about Crosby's decision to take the slapshot.

"His slap shot is, uhh, not that good," said Malkin. "That shot he just put everything in it, all the motion, all the power and he shot that puck that hard."

For game two, the Rangers succeeded in part in shutting down the Penguins offense, but in doing so they completely forgot the offense of their own as goaltender Marc-Andre Fleury continued his stellar play, shutting out the Rangers 2–0.

Game three was more of the same from the Penguins, as the Rangers could not figure out how to gain the advantage on the youthful legs of the Pens. All the Penguins needed was one more win to be one series away from the big show.

Facing intense pressure at home, the Rangers had to play their best hockey of the season in order to stay alive. If they failed, it might be the last time the fans at Madison Square Garden would see their captain Jaromir Jagr in a Rangers jersey, as his impending free agency put his future with the club in jeopardy. As it turned out, the captain gave his fans a great show, scoring two goals and getting an assist on the third to lift the Rangers to victory. For the first time in the 2008 playoffs, the Penguins showed they were human.

Crosby was pretty quiet in the series, with just four assists, but the young phenom had to deal with rigorous checking and verbal jabs from the Rangers' veteran players. At times he showed that he was still a young player getting his feet wet in the pressure cooker of the playoffs, but then there were the times when he could simply astound. Like the man he is most often compared to (Wayne Gretzky, in case you didn't know), Crosby might not always get the goals, but it is his consistent effort and drive to score goals that make him an incredible player, and everyone around him even better. He proved it in game five when he led the Pens up the ice midway through the second period and assisted on the opening goal by Marian Hossa. The Pens were determined to finish off the series, peppering Ranger goaltender Henrik Lundqvist with 17 shots in the second period alone, while the Rangers could muster only four. Malkin put the Penguins ahead by two goals in the last half of the second, and it seemed as though the Rangers would be heading for the golf courses soon. But in the third period they got two quick goals and managed to hold on, sending the game into overtime.

In overtime, Captain Crosby took over. At the seven-minute mark of the first overtime period, he led the rush into the Rangers zone with Pascal Dupuis and Marian Hossa at his side. Crossing into the zone, Crosby hit Dupuis with a pass, and Dupuis shot it back to Crosby, but the puck trickled off his stick and luckily found its way to Hossa, who scored the series winner at 7:10 of overtime.

"Sid was driving hard to the net and it kind of bounced off him, and the puck just came up to me, and I just tried to shoot at the net—and it was a lucky one," Hossa said. Dispensing of the highly touted veteran squad like the Rangers, the Penguins proved that a group of young guys could come together to face any challenge. But Crosby admitted that his team still needed to learn a few things before they could lift the Cup. "We knew we had a special group here, and a young group that just needed to get experience. We're still learning a lot," Crosby said.

Next Up: Philadelphia Flyers

"You want a rivalry, there's one right there. It doesn't get any easier," Crosby said of the often rough and action-packed season series in which Philadelphia won five of eight and the Eastern Conference finals.

The Flyers might have won five of eight during the regular season, but this was the playoffs, and none of those games counted now. The only thing that carried over from the regular season was the bad blood. Since 1967, when the two Pennsylvania state teams entered into the NHL, they had never really been the best of friends, and the bad blood continued into the Conference finals in 2008.

"We know they will target guys like Crosby and Malkin and Hossa and (Petr) Sykora, but that's fine," said Penguins head coach Michel Therrien. "That's the playoffs. Ottawa tried to do it. The Rangers tried to do it."

Crosby himself was no stranger to the "brotherly" love dealt out by the Philadelphia Flyers; he had received several chipped teeth and a bloody mouth courtesy of Flyer defenseman Darian Hatcher in 2005. But Crosby showed the Flyers his own form of bad blood by scoring 37 points in 20 career games against Philly, so the 2008 series promised to be a good one for the fans of both teams.

Game one of the Eastern Conference finals at Mellon Arena was a raucous affair, and the Penguins burst out onto the ice to hear the deafening cheer from their fans all dressed in white. Looking at the stands from afar, the fans appeared as one in a sea of cheering white that ebbed and flowed with the fortunes of their boys on the ice. The Penguins Petr Sykora answered the prayers of fans when he broke the ice with a beautiful goal scored along the goal line by switching from his forehand to his backhand to beat Flyers goaltender Martin Biron. Mike Richards took the life out of the crowd soon after with two goals before the clock reached the halfway mark of the first period. Then came time for Crosby to come out of his shell. For the past five games the Penguin captain had been held scoreless, but two minutes after the Flyers' second goal, Crosby took a beautiful pass from linemate Marian Hossa and cut in from the right circle to put the puck in past Biron. Evgeni Malkin took over from there with two spectacular goals to put the Penguins out of reach by a score of 4–2.

Philadelphia Flyers head coach John Stevens was not happy after the game and knew exactly why they had lost the game. "You turn pucks over and give up rushes against Crosby and Malkin, that's a game you can't play."

The problem for Stevens was that the Flyers did not learn anything from game one and lost game two by exactly the same score. Leading the Penguins to yet another home victory was their captain Sidney Crosby with one goal, an assist and the first star of the game to his credit.

Back home in Philadelphia, the Flyers were hoping that their fans could give them that extra boost they needed to get back into the series. While the Mellon Arena in Pittsburgh had their whiteout, the Flyers faithful had their orange crush to help propel their team to victory. It had worked against the Washington Capitals and the

Montreal Canadiens, but for game three, the sea of orange at Wachovia Center could do little to stem the tide of the Penguin attack.

Captain Sidney Crosby again led his squad on the attack with two assists, but it was his consistency and aggressiveness on the puck that showed his teammates that their leader was never going to give up. Marian Hossa might have got two goals, but it was because of the work of his captain that he even had the opportunity. The Flyers fans had only one goal by forward R. J. Umberger to cheer about, and they left Wachovia with their heads down with a 4–1 loss to contemplate—one loss away from seeing their favorite players on the golf course rather than on the ice.

For game four, the Flyers finally learned from their mistakes, with a 4–2 victory of their own, but that was just delaying the inevitable. Game five proved to be the Flyers' last hurrah in the 2008 playoffs as Crosby and the gang pounded six goals over Philadelphia, who did not manage to get one past Marc-Andre Fleury. This was the young team that no one thought would make it far into the playoffs and who one year earlier had exited the playoffs in the first round.

On presentation of the Conference championship trophy, Sidney Crosby posed for photos but dared not touch the trophy. "We all realized it's not the one we want to be holding," said Crosby after the game. By superstition, most team captains refuse to handle any trophy other than the Stanley Cup. The Penguins' biggest challenge yet would be in the next round against the regular season champs, the Detroit Red Wings.

The Final Round: Detroit Red Wings

After nearly a week off while waiting for the Detroit Red Wings to finish off the Dallas Stars, "Sid the Kid" was ready to take on hockey town. Pittsburgh was alive with excitement, because the last time their boys in black and gold had been in the finals was when Mario the Magnificent led the Pens to their second straight Stanley Cup in 1992, a legacy that Crosby would have surely liked to leave on the city.

The NHL could not have asked for a better match-up than the Pittsburgh Penguins and the Detroit Red Wings. The two teams had an equal amount of scoring talent (Crosby, Malkin and Hossa for the Penguins; and Datsyuk, Zetterberg and Frazen for the Wings), two solid defenses (Hal Gill and Sergei Gonchar for the Pens; and Nicklas Lidstrom and Brian Rafalski for the Wings) and two reliable goaltenders (Marc-Andre Fleury for the Pens; and Chris Osgood for the Wings.) This would be the young Penguins captain's biggest challenge in his brief yet illustrious career. Crosby already had a scoring title and an MVP award on his shelf, and now he wanted the biggest trophy around.

Detroit Red Wing captain Nicklas Lidstrom knew that anticipation for this series was high and expectations were even higher. "The skill level is going to be very high," Lidstrom said. "That's one of the reasons a lot of people wanted this kind of matchup. People were talking about it in the media before we got here. A lot of people wanted to see two highly skilled teams, two offensive teams, two puck possession teams in the finals."

For the first time in the 2008 playoffs, the Penguins had to start off without the support of the Penguins whiteout and with a less than warm reception from the Hockeytown faithful. But it wasn't only the fans of the two teams who were watching the game. Television ratings in the United States for the games leading up to the finals hadn't been this high since the 2002–03 playoffs, and the final in 2008 with the NHL's biggest draw, Sidney Crosby, promised to bring in many more new fans. The Conference finals alone had increased viewership, up 71 percent from the previous year, and the Stanley Cup finals promised to be even better. The new popularity of the sport in the U.S. was not lost on Crosby. "I don't think as a player you can worry about that a whole lot," Crosby said. "I mean you do your best to help your team win, and I think that's where most guys' focus is. You can't control the other stuff. If that's the case, then great. That's great for the game and great for everyone involved."

Even NBC sportscaster Mike Emrick was aware of the significance of this high-profile series. "I cannot recall more stars in a final since 1987, when Edmonton had five of the best, but they were all on one team," he said. "This time we have the stars divided out on teams. The hockey gods are smiling so wide, we can count their missing teeth."

There was a lot of hype surrounding the start of the Stanley Cup finals, and Detroit's Joe Louis Arena was buzzing with anticipation. Sidney Crosby stepped out onto the ice for the start of the game and in doing so realized his dream of playing for the Stanley Cup. All those days of waking up early at 5:00 AM, all the bumps, bruises and countless frustrations were finally paying off. But like any true warrior athlete, Crosby still wasn't satisfied with a trip into the finals.

If the first period of game one was any indication of how the series would progress, then the fans were in for a treat. The pace was fast; the hits were heavy; and both goaltenders were busy blocking an equal amount of shots. Although no goals were scored in the first period, it was some of the best hockey of the year. Into the second period, Pittsburgh looked like a completely different team. They only managed four shots on net, and the normally young offensive core was stymied by the veteran Detroit defense. The Penguins only managed 19 shots in total and could not find the handle to put one behind Chris Osgood. Detroit, on the other hand, easily showed why they were the best team during the regular season, displaying excellent puck control and clinical execution of their system. The Penguins had no chance, and that was reflected in the 4–0 final score. Penguins head coach Michel Therrien knew his team deserved to lose after putting in that kind of performance. "I don't know if it was the nerves," Therrien said. "Definitely that was the worst performance of the playoffs. We didn't compete like we were supposed to compete. It's a good lesson."

Crosby tried to put a more positive spin on the negative outcome. "I don't think we came here expecting an easy series," Crosby said. "For sure they played a tight checking game. That's playoff hockey. You still have to find ways around that."

It's nice to say you need to do things differently in order to win, but it's another thing to actually do them. In game two, the Red Wings had an answer for everything the Penguins tried to do differently, and the frustration was beginning to show. Max Talbot and Gary Roberts took 14 minutes in penalties each, and the Penguins spent a total of 44 minutes with a man in the box while the Red Wings only rode the pine for a total of 16 minutes. If Detroit could continue that style of play, then the Penguins were in for an early exit. The key for Detroit lay in stifling the Penguins' captain, and Henrik Zetterberg was doing an excellent job of keeping Sidney away from the net and keeping him plenty frustrated. Being the home team, the Red Wings enjoyed the privilege of last change, and every time Crosby stepped out on the ice, Wings head coach Mike Babcock simply put on the Zetterberg line. It was a frustrating game for Crosby, who is normally used to getting a little more space on the ice than Zetterberg was allowing.

"They do a good job of definitely clogging up the neutral zone and holding up," Crosby said. "As players, you have to battle through that sometimes and hope they get the calls."

The Red Wings were so good in the second game that their third and fourth line players were getting the goals, and by the end of game two the Penguins had yet to score in the series, while Detroit was just two victories away from taking the series after a 3–0 win. In order for the Penguins to win, their captain had to figure out how to solve the Wings defense and score a goal. The one good thing was that the Pens would finally be in front of their home crowd, a place where they had not lost a single game during the entire playoffs.

Game three was the type of match-up everyone was hoping to see. Fast paced, plenty of scoring chances, few whistles and some amazing saves. By the midway point of the first period, Mellon Arena was so loud that the television announcers had to scream so that the people at home could hear what they were saying. The roof almost lifted off when Marian Hossa intercepted a weak Detroit clearing attempt and blasted a shot at Osgood that hit a defenseman in front and found its way onto the stick of Sidney Crosby. Crosby snapped it in for the Penguins' first goal of the series at the 17:25 mark of the first period.

"Whether it was me or anybody else, we just wanted to get the first one," Crosby said. "We wanted to get a goal, find a way. That was the mind-set going in, and it was nice to get it for sure."

But the Penguins captain still had more to give. Two minutes into the second period, with the Penguins on a power play, Crosby parked himself beside the Wings net and was rewarded for his patience when a Sergei Gonchar blast from the point deflected onto his stick for the easy tap in, right into the wide open net, and just like that the Pens had a 2–0 lead. The Wings managed to put a good scare into Penguins fans when Johan Franzen scored to put Detroit within reach, but later in the third period the Penguins pulled away for good when Adam Hall popped in a goal off Chris Osgood's skate for a 3–1 lead. It was all the Penguins needed to get themselves back into the series. Detroit scored one in the late stages of the third period but could not put anything extra past Fleury. With the series now at 2–1, the Penguins were feeling a little more optimistic about their chances.

"Look at it. We're one game away from tying up the Stanley Cup finals, after a lot of you guys counted us out," said Penguins defenseman Ryan Whitney.

But the Pens were still far away from their goal. This was only one win, and if they wanted three more, they were going to need every player at their best and not just Crosby. And the veteran Detroit squad was too experienced to let one simple win get them off their game.

Game four saw the Red Wings tighten up on defense and give little if any chances for Pittsburgh's top line to score. Although Pittsburgh did score the first goal of the game (with an assist for Captain Crosby), it was a tight defensive affair from there on in, and Detroit won the game 2–1 on the strength of goals by Nicklas Lidstrom and Jiri Hudler and the near flawless goaltending by Chris Osgood.

All Detroit needed was one more win to have their 11th Cup in franchise history. Crosby's dreams of hoisting the Stanley Cup were quickly fading. Odds were heavily stacked against the Pens, and they needed a near miracle to pull off three straight wins over the Red Wings.

For Crosby, the series was coming down to a period-by period, shift-by-shift attitude; win the small battles and the war will follow. "We have to win one to get back," Crosby said. "That's the way we're thinking. They scored two, we scored one, so I don't think they're running away with it. We'll battle them in Detroit and see what happens."

Game five truly was a battle. It had all the elements of a classic game: the Stanley Cup on the line, back and forth scoring, intense physical play and the greatest goaltending performance of the 2008 playoffs by Marc-Andre Fleury. For most of the game it looked as if the Penguins were a few unlucky bounces from losing the game, but the puck seemed to favor the sticks of the Pens that night.

Marian Hossa opened up the scoring when he took a pass from Crosby and blasted it by a sprawling Chris Osgood. The Penguins' second goal of the game was credited to Adam Hall, but he had Red Wings defenseman Niklas Kronwall to thank for it. Driving to the net and creating a mass of confusion, Hall got the puck to the front of the net, but it was out of reach to make a play. In a panic to clear the puck, Kronwall shot it off Hall's skate and passed Osgood another Penguins goal. The goal was particularly deflating for the Red Wings, as it seemed they were getting the most chances on the Penguins net, but nothing was working for them. That is, until the Wings' constant pressure finally paid off in three unanswered goals, and with 10 minutes remaining in the game, the Penguins found that their season was on the brink, down 3–2. In the hallways of Joe Louis Arena, the Stanley Cup was removed from its protective case and bottles of champagne were put on ice. With one minute remaining in the game, Detroit fans watched with bated breath as each second seemed to slowly peel itself off the clock.

In the final flurry in front of Chris Osgood in goal, the Penguins tried everything they could to get the puck into the net. Finally, the puck took one lucky bounce and ended up on the stick of Max Talbot, who slid the puck past Osgood on the left side with a few seconds left on the clock. The collective wind was knocked out of Joe Louis Arena as the puck crossed the line. Assisting on the play were Marian Hossa and the captain Sidney Crosby. The Penguins once again had life in their skates, but the game was far from done; overtime was just around the corner, and the Red Wings were out for revenge.

For the overtime, Crosby was the Red Wings' primary target. The young captain barely had a chance to get away from the tight checking of Zetterberg and proved ineffective through the overtime. The Red Wings put on a clinic of professional hockey skills. Exiting their zone was flawless, movement through the neutral zone was perfect, and their setup in enemy territory was effortless, but the only problem was that Marc-Andre Fleury kept stopping their shots. One overtime went by, then another, and finally into the third overtime, Petr Sykora scored the game-winning goal on a power play. The Penguins were still alive, thanks to a few timely goals and, most of all, to Fleury.

For Crosby, despite the Pens still being down in the series, he was exactly where he wanted to be at that moment. "We're still here, still battling, and we still have an opportunity here," he said. And that's all that mattered, having that chance.

Back in Pittsburgh, the Penguins were hoping that with a little crowd support and a little luck, they could send the series back to Detroit and have one more shot at the Cup. This was exactly where the Red Wings did not want to be, and Crosby was hoping to take advantage. Mellon Arena was jumping with energy as the Penguins hit the ice before the start of the game. Mario Lemieux sat in his private box with his wife and close friends, gazing down on the young team he helped to build and mold, hoping once again to see the Cup in Pittsburgh. But those dreams were quickly wiped away as the Detroit Red Wings put in two goals before the game was even half over. There was a feeling in the building that this might be the Penguins' swan song. Evgeni Malkin's power-play goal before the end of the second period brought some life back into the building, but it was quickly extinguished when Zetterberg put the Wings ahead 3–1. With time ticking away on the Red Wings' season, Jiri Hudler took a hooking penalty and gave the Penguins the opportunity they needed to get back into the game. Marian Hossa brought them back to life when he deflected a Sergei Gonchar point shot past Chris Osgood. A sense of possibility flooded the arena that the Penguins could actually tie up the game in the dying seconds, just as they had done two days earlier.

Head coach Michel Therrien pulled goaltender Marc-Andre Fleury and threw on his best players for a last-minute Hail Mary play. Hossa had the best chance when Crosby got the puck on his stick and sent it inches from the goal line with a few seconds left. The final buzzer sounded, and the Detroit Red Wings were crowned the Stanley Cup champions. Crosby politely shook the hands of his conqueror and skated off the ice without garnering a single trophy. Henrik Zetterberg won the Conn Smythe Trophy, most likely for his role in keeping Crosby at bay when it counted most. Although the Penguins managed to put up a fight, the Detroit Red Wings' experience and leadership propelled them through the difficult moments all the way to the Cup.

***

For Sidney Crosby, the loss was a painful outcome to swallow. He had physically, mentally and emotionally prepared for that moment all his life, and to have it taken away in six games was difficult to accept. So much pressure had been placed on his shoulders, and despite scoring six goals and 21 assists (tying Henrik Zetterberg in the leading playoff scorers), Crosby still managed to garner some criticism for his level of play on the ice. But if you consider his age and the energy he brings to each game, night in and night out, Crosby is only guilty of a few slight lapses. You have to forgive a player for a minor slip when it is through his brilliance that the Penguins had persevered and took game three to give the Penguins some hope.

After only his third year in the NHL, Sidney Crosby managed to come back from a mid-season injury to lead his teammates through a final run of wins in the regular season, smashing through their Eastern Conference rivals and taking a young team close to hockey immortality. Credit must be given where credit is due; after all, Wayne Gretzky won the Stanley Cup only in his fifth year with the Edmonton Oilers. Crosby had just played his third. The tension will keep us watching.

Just a few years into his NHL career, Sidney Crosby has helped the league return from obscurity after the NHL lockout to the success of today. His leadership and vision on the ice helped to elevate the Penguins out of the basement of the league in just one season to become one of the best and most dynamic teams in the Eastern Conference. Throughout his life he has constantly been compared to other players, but the time for comparisons should end, because Sidney Crosby has already made a name for himself.

Chapter Eleven

Redemption

Over the summer all he could think about was how close he'd come. It had been his lifelong dream to make it into the Stanley Cup finals, and to have it slip away in the final was tough. The 2007–08 season was one of triumphs and tribulations, coming back from injury, making it into the finals past some tough opponents, only to have the Stanley Cup wrenched away when it was just within reach. The summer was filled with off-season training, visiting family and friends and simply recovering and building toward the upcoming season.

During the off-season, the Penguins scoring attack took a hit when Marion Hossa decided to jump ship to the team that had just defeated them. It was clear that Hossa was looking to put a Stanley Cup on his resume, and he felt his chances were better with the Red Wings organization. For Crosby, the departure of Hossa took him by surprise.

"When it did first happen, I was pretty surprised," Crosby told ESPN.com. "I thought he was coming back. There wasn't a big question in my mind; I was looking forward to playing with him again. It was just a matter of how long was he going to sign for. But then, as things developed, I found out other teams were in the mix. So when he didn't sign, it's nothing personal."

Crosby tried not to take it personally, but it was impossible to ignore the fact that Hossa had simply chosen Detroit because he felt he had a better chance with them than with the Penguins. As the captain and face of the team it was something of a burn, but hockey goes on and so did Crosby and the Penguins. And the best revenge is to win hockey games.

Early in the season on October 18, 2008, Crosby potted a goal and three assists to all at once surpass the benchmarks of 100 goals, 200 assists and 300 points. It also just so happened that on the same play in which Crosby scored, Evgeni Malkin got his own 200th point of his career. Pittsburgh's young guns sent notice to the league that the Penguins were ready to do battle.

But the initial surge by the Penguins' top players failed to inspire the rest of the team, and head coach Michel Therrien seemed to be fumbling for solutions to their problems. It was embarrassing to the team to come so close to winning the Cup and then to be on the razor's edge of missing the playoffs the next year. But it was an embarrassment that the Penguins' management was not going to allow to continue. As often happens when a team needs to refocus its efforts, the head coach is first on the chopping block.

"I didn't like the way, the direction the team was headed," said general manager Ray Shero in a conference call, not long after giving Therrien the news. "I've watched for a number of weeks and, at the end of the day, the direction is not what I wanted to have here. I wasn't comfortable, and that's why the change was made."

Therrien operated under a system where every player was responsible for playing a tight defensive game. But with such offensively skilled players as Sidney Crosby and Evgeni Malkin, it was hard to force some players into those roles, and the dressing room rebelled against Therrien's efforts. Shero turned to former NHL player and coach of Pittsburgh's farm team, Dan Bylsma, to get the team back on track. For the new NHL coach it was clear what he needed to do from the beginning.

"With the strengths we have, we should be able to go into buildings and make teams deal with the quality of players we have at every position," Bylsma said. "I look at a group that can win games right now, and we need to do that. We can do this, but the players have to believe we can do this."

The response from the players was immediate. Play on the ice opened up, and the Pens best players started to light up the scoreboard. The Penguins finished the regular season 4th in the Eastern Conference and earned home ice advantage over their first-round opponents, the Philadelphia Flyers. The Pens captain finished out the season in style with 33 goals and 70 assists, and Evgeni Malkin captured the league scoring race, beating out fellow Russian sniper Alexander Ovechkin for the Art Ross Trophy.

Philadelphia looked for revenge against the Penguins after a physical series in the 2008 playoffs that got them knocked out in an embarrassing five games. None other than Sidney Crosby got the series off to a wild start by scoring a power play goal early in the first period of game one and leading the way to a 4–1 victory. The Flyers wanted revenge for the previous year's elimination, but their zeal cost them dearly in the penalty department, having to kill off 12 minor infractions in game one alone.

In game two the Flyers seemed to wake up but still managed to lose in overtime when veteran Bill Guerin scored the winner in overtime to put the Pens up two games to nothing. Marc-Andre Fleury had a rough game three and let the Flyers steal one by a score of 6–3. But the flexible French-Canadian goaltender bounced back and led the Pens through to a 3–1 win in game four to take the crucial 3–1 lead in the series. The Flyers worked hard in game five to stave off elimination and road the incredible goaltending of Martin Biron to shut out the Pens 3–0 and bring the series to 3 games to 2.

The Flyers felt the series turn around and knew if they could jump out to an early lead at the start of game six, they might be able to force a seventh game. By the second period the Flyers had stuck to their game plan and put up three unanswered goals. The Pens appeared down and out and needing a boost. Max Talbot answered the team's need by dropping the goals with heavyweight Dan Carcillo for an even bout that energized the crowd and lit a fire beneath the Penguins' offense. In the third period, the Penguins scored five unanswered goals including two from their captain. The Penguins won the series and moved on to the next challenge.

Up next was the series that everyone had been anticipating since Sidney Crosby and Alexander Ovechkin joined the NHL. Questions, criticisms and commentary flew through the media days before the teams even played one minute of the series. Who was the better player? Who was the better leader? Who would emerge in the end with the title of the greatest player in the NHL? This was the NHL's dream series match-up, and win or lose, the fans were in for a rollercoaster ride.

Washington had just been through a difficult physical series with the New York Rangers and had come back from a 3–1 series deficit to win the series in seven games. The Capitals had proven themselves and were expecting to ride the wave of excitement into the series against Crosby led by their own top man, Alex Ovechkin. The series even had Don Cherry worked into a frenzy, calling Crosby and Ovechkin the most complete hockey players in the game and able to lead their teams to the Cup. There was no doubt in anyone's mind that this would be a classic hockey battle, and the two powerhouse teams did not disappoint.

Game one in Washington's Verizon Center saw a stunning performance from Capitals rookie goaltender. Simeon Varlamov kept the Penguins offense at bay, making 34 saves for a 3–2 victory. Crosby got a goal in the game, but was frustrated all night by the acrobatic saves of the Capitals goalie.

"He gave us a chance to win the game," Washington superstar Alex Ovechkin said of his rookie goaltender.

If ever hockey games could be called masterpieces, then game two of the Washington-Pittsburgh series would be the Mona Lisa. It had everything you could wish for in a hockey game—amazing goaltending, well-executed passing, energy and most of all, the game's two brightest superstars in a head-to-head battle of skill, leadership and pure scoring ability.

First on the scoreboard was Crosby, giving the Penguins a 1–0 lead by the six-minute mark of the first period, and Marc-Andre Fleury was able to keep the team ahead by the end of the first. But the Penguins couldn't keep Ovechkin locked in all night, and at the two-minute mark of the second period, the sniper blasted a one-timer off a sweet pass from Victor Kozlov. But Crosby answered the challenge with another goal, his second of the night, at 10:57 of the second.

However, while Crosby had all the answers, his teammates had not added a single point. Ovechkin on the other hand got a little help from his friends when, not five minutes after Crosby gave the Pens the 2–1 lead, the Caps David Steckel scored to tie the game. After Steckel's interruption, the Crosby-Ovechkin show continued into the third period.

Ovechkin was the first to strike with another one-timer that found a hole between Fleury's pads to put the Caps up 3–2. The Verizon Center burst with cheers of "MVP! MVP! MVP!" from the 18,277 fans dressed in Capital red. Two minutes later, Ovechkin ripped another shot past Fleury for the hat trick and a 4–2 lead.

Time was running out, and Crosby, as the Penguins' leader, knew he had to step up yet again if his team was going to pull out the win.

Crosby knew that the best place for him to be was down low in front of the goaltender. It was how he had beaten Varlamov for the two previous goals, and with just 30 seconds left in the period, Crosby got four whacks at the puck before he pushed it past the rookie goalie for his own hat trick. But it was too little, too late. In the battle of Crosby vs. Ovechkin, this game went to the Capitals sniper. But for Crosby, the war was still on.

The Pens put themselves back into the series with a 3–2 overtime victory before a relieved hometown crowd at Mellon Arena. Crosby assisted defenseman Kris Letang on the play at 11:23 of the first overtime period. When backed into a corner, the Penguins captain did what he had done his entire hockey playing career: he fought back. The Penguins took the next game, again led by Crosby who garnered first star honors, potting one goal and two assists in a 5–3 Pittsburgh-dominated game.

"I think that our consistency wasn't there for the most part in the first two games, and we did make big mistakes," Crosby said after the game. "If we did make a mistake in the [last two games] we found a way to get ourselves out of it."

In game five, Crosby did not register a point, but his teammates stepped up to the plate with a 4–3 overtime win. But in game six, the Capitals were able to pull another win out of the Pens hands with a 5–4 overtime victory. It seemed almost natural that the series would extend to a seventh game because both Crosby and Ovechkin are competitors first, and neither was going down without a fight. But game seven was somewhat anticlimactic. Fans and media expected another classic battle where Sidney scored a goal only to be matched by Ovechkin's brilliance. Instead, Caps rookie goaltender Varlamov had a bad start, and the Penguins pulled out to a quick 4–0 lead. The Caps pulled Varlamov in hopes of stemming the bleeding, but the Penguins scored two more goals to finish off the series with a 6–2 victory. Crosby scored two more goals and added an assist to finish this one series alone with 13 points. Ovechkin ended up with one more point in the series than Crosby. Up next, Carolina.

The conference finals against the Carolina Hurricanes began with a close game one—a 3–2 victory for the Penguins—and it only got easier as the Canes went down in four games straight. Crosby then had to wait for the results of the Detroit Red Wings–Chicago Blackhawks conference final to see who he would face for the Cup. Part of him must have been hoping the Red Wings would win, so that he would get the chance to face down his old teammate Marion Hossa and show him he bet on the wrong team.

"You can tell they won it last year, and they wanted a chance to do it again," Carolina Hurricanes forward Scott Walker said, speaking first about the conference championship and then the Stanley Cup. "I wouldn't want to be facing them if I was on one of the other two teams (remaining in the West)."

As fate would have it, the Red Wings came out on top in the series against the Blackhawks. Crosby and the Pens would have the chance to taste revenge. But the Red Wings were no push-overs and wanted to prove again that they could stop the great Crosby. After the first two games of the final and two 3–1 losses, it looked like Crosby and the Penguins were about to fold under the pressure. In the locker room, after the end of the second loss, the Penguins struggled to find an answer to why they were not putting up wins.

"We had stretches where we played good. We got scoring chances and pucks around the net. Didn't capitalize on them when they need to, and they got timely goals and goals in around our net and end up with the victory," said Pens head coach, Dan Bylsma.

But as was the case in the Washington series, the Penguins returned home, refocused and fed off the incredible energy of the fans to pull out back-to-back wins to tie the series. Crosby and Malkin had regained their scoring touch, and best of all, Fleury had regained his confidence.

Evgeni Malkin summed up the Penguins philosophy after the game with a few poignant words. "I don't seek points. I want to the win Stanley Cup."

Plans for that Stanley Cup had to be put on hold in game five when the Red Wings had an incredible game led by the goaltending of veteran Chris Osgood, while the Pens' Fleury got the hook after the Red Wings fifth goal of the game. Down three games to two in the series, the Penguins needed to work hard, and they needed a little luck to pull out the series win.

In the last two games of the series, the glory did not belong to Sidney Crosby or Evgeni Malkin but to the Pens support staff, and they got the job done. Marc-Andre Fluery put on an incredible display of clutch goaltending, turning aside 26 shots in game six to lead the Pens to a close 2–1 victory, and more importantly, a shot at a seventh game in the Stanley Cup finals.

"I think that's the storyline of the playoffs, when your team can play well enough that different people can put on the cape on any given night," said Pens coach, Dan Bylsma.

Crosby and the Pens had the momentum, but they knew very well what the Red Wings were capable of, and they would have to try and beat them before a hometown crowd. The pressure was on, and even the best players felt it.

"I'd always like to score more," said Crosby, who had a goal and two assists in the series.

"I look back, and on some of the chances I've had just didn't really get a whole lot of luck. Now is not the time to think about what could have been. The only way I'm looking at here is it's a great opportunity, and I've got to try to go out there and play my best game in the playoffs."

But it wasn't Crosby who had the best game of his playoffs; it was Maxime Talbot. A third- or fourth-line tough guy, Talbot was the Penguins energy player, called on to provide the team with a lift when needed—he was not hired to score goals. That night, however, Talbot scored two of the most important goals of his career, potting the Penguins first and second goals in the second period. The Red Wings tried to answer by attacking the net directly, but Fleury would not allow anything by, and at the end of second the Penguins had a 2–0 lead. The Red Wings Jonathan Ericsson gave his team some hope at the 14-minute mark of the third, blasting a shot past Fleury, but it was all they could muster. Not even a last second desperation shot by captain Nick Lidstrom could solve Marc Andre Fleury.

The third period siren sounded, and the Penguins bench erupted. Sidney Crosby had led his team to the Stanley Cup, making him the youngest captain ever to win the trophy. The saddest man in the building surely had to be

Marion Hossa, who had gambled on Detroit's fortunes and ended up betting on the wrong horse.

"I would have loved to do it in four [games], it would have been a lot easier on the nerves," said Crosby. "It was so hard watching the clock tick down for that whole third period. But everything it took to win, we did it, you know. Blocking shots. Great goaltending. Different guys stepping up. I mean, we did exactly everything it takes to win. We're really happy with the result. We've been through a lot."

Captain Crosby received the Cup from NHL commissioner Gary Bettman and lifted it over his head for real this time. Countless times he had played this moment over and over in his head, and now he had done it. He was Sidney Crosby, Stanley Cup Champion.

Chapter Twelve

Summer with the Cup

After raising the Stanley Cup above his head and enjoying every moment of the celebration with his teammates on the ice of Joe Louis Arena, Sidney Crosby's summer was just beginning.

Just three days later, the championship team returned home to Pittsburgh to celebrate with their fans. Tens of thousands lined the streets to show their team and captain just how much they appreciated their efforts. Pittsburgh sports fans were a little spoiled that year since their Pittsburgh Steelers had also won their league championship just five months earlier. All that celebrating lifted the spirits of the city and showed the fans' pride for their Penguins in bringing the Stanley Cup back to Pittsburgh for the first time since 1991. When Crosby appeared in the parade brandishing the Cup high above his head, the crowd went wild for their captain. Sitting quietly behind

Sidney in the car were his parents, Troy and Trina, also beaming with pride. After the parade, Crosby stood on stage in front of the thousands of Penguins supporters and addressed the crowd.

"We want to go for more," Crosby said to the crowd, eliciting a flurry of screams. "I just want to say it was a privilege and an honor to go through this with everyone. We've all dreamed of doing this, and let's do it again some other time."

Crosby had certainly come a long way from the eager 14-year-old that once told a CBC reporter, "Getting up everyday and doing something that you love to do, and just, like, enjoying it, even getting paid to do something that you love to do I can't even imagine how amazing that would be."

In his fantasies as a 14-year-old, he had certainly played out winning the Stanley Cup many times, but the reality of the moment was far better than even he could ever have imagined. Once the parade was over and the parties in Pittsburgh had wrapped up, it was time for Sidney to get his day with the Cup. And there was just one place he could think of to take it—where that 14-year-old kid's dreams began. The day after he won the Cup, Sidney and his parents called a close family friend back home in Cole Harbour, Nova Scotia, and asked him to organize a little welcome-home gathering. The date Crosby selected to return home with the Cup? None other than August 7, Sidney's birthday.

But this was not going to be some hastily thrown-together parade down the streets of his childhood neighborhood. Crosby knew exactly what he wanted to do that day. This celebration might never come again in his career, and he knew that the event should celebrate the people and places that made him the person and the player he was. The Crosbys counted on family friend Paul Mason for the task of organizing the celebration, and Mason told Paul Hollingsworth in his book *Sidney Crosby: The Story of a Champion* that from the outset, Crosby had a plan for the day.

"When I met him and talked to him about how it would go, he already had a set idea of how it would go with every detail. He wanted to go to the hospital and meet with the kids. He wanted the ground hockey game with his friends. There was never any question that it would be based out of his home community of Cole Harbour."

On the morning of his birthday, Crosby awoke early and headed out to the airport to await the arrival of the Stanley Cup by private jet. Phil Pritchard, Keeper of the Cup, handed over the Canadian treasure to Crosby, and he was immediately whisked off by the Canadian military in a Sea King helicopter for a rendezvous with the HMCS *Preserver*. There, thousands of fans, friends, former coaches, Canada's military servicemen and women and even National Minister of Defence Peter MacKay awaited his arrival.

Crosby's father, Troy, commented on the reason for the military visit: "He's a proud Canadian, and he understands the sacrifices that these men and women do." After signing as many autographs as he could and taking pictures with families, Crosby and the Cup were off to their next destination.

Giving back to his community has always been important to Crosby, and he did not hesitate to take the Cup to the IWK Health Centre in Halifax to share it with the sick children and their parents, bringing smiles to their faces. He spent time talking with the kids and their parents, signing more autographs and taking pictures.

From there, it was off to his old neighborhood, where he paraded down the street, riding in a vintage fire truck flanked by a dozen members of the Royal Canadian Mounted Police in full ceremonial uniform. Seeing all the people who turned out to support him and the level of excitement, Crosby could not help but shed tears of joy—definitely unexpected from the normally composed young man, but understandable given the emotions of the day. Phil Pritchard, curator of the Hockey Hall of Fame, Keeper of the Stanley Cup and the man whose job it is to travel with the Cup wherever it goes, was in attendance for the parade and could not believe that so many people turned out for the Crosby celebration.

"I've been traveling with the Cup 21 years, and I don't think there has been a party this big for an individual player," said Pritchard. Thousands of fans packed the streets of Cole Harbour, waving Penguins jerseys, holding up signs and applauding their hometown boy.

Crosby could hardly believe his eyes when he saw the crowd. "People here are unbelievable. I think you see how lucky I am with the amount of support that's here, so that pretty much says it all."

The parade ended with a rally at a local park where Sidney and his teammate Max Talbot addressed the crowd and thanked them for their overwhelming support. He then played a not-so-private game of roller hockey with some of his closest friends while several hundred spectators watched from the sidelines. At the conclusion of the game, friends and family retired to the Crosby household for a private party.

The next morning, when one of the Keepers of the Cup arrived to take it to the next player for

their day, Sidney requested the privilege of clean-
ing the Cup. After a good scrubbing, Crosby
reluctantly handed over the trophy, and his time
with the Stanley Cup was done. He had just a few
fleeting moments with that Canadian treasure,
but he will have the memories to last a lifetime,
as will the thousands of hometown hockey fans
he shared it with. But Sidney Crosby was not yet
finished in the memories department because
in just a few short months, he would make
hockey history.

Chapter Thirteen

A Legend is Born

The 2009–10 season began with the defending Stanley Cup champions raising their third Stanley Cup banner to the rafters of Mellon Arena. It was a wonderful summer for the team and for Crosby; they were finally able to savor the sweet taste of victory after recalling their last summer off in 2008 when they lost the Cup in the finals to the Detroit Red Wings. The season began with incredible expectations placed on Crosby and his Penguins given that the winning team had remained largely intact through the summer free agent frenzy and flurry of trades. They clearly had a well-rounded team, and with the thrill of the Stanley Cup victory still buzzing, many sports writers picked the Penguins to repeat as champions. The only thing that could keep them from winning was complacency, but with a captain like Sidney Crosby, who doesn't know the meaning of the word, the season appeared filled with possibilities.

Throughout the first half of the season, despite a few ups and downs, the Penguins appeared on track for a winning finish. Crosby had his highs and lows in the first 41 games, going on a five-game pointless streak, the worst of his young career. Eventually, the goals started coming, and the Penguins concluded the first half of the season with a record of 26–14–1. The young Captain also managed a few milestones in those first 41 games, becoming the sixth fastest player to score 400 points. He also scored his 150th career goal on December 3 against the Colorado Avalanche. The big question at that point in the season was whether or not Crosby and the Penguins could muster enough energy in the grueling NHL schedule, especially with the Vancouver 2010 Olympics just around the corner.

The National Hockey League had come to an agreement with the Olympics committee that it would shut down operations for three weeks to allow its best and brightest from all over the world to travel to Vancouver for a chance to represent their countries on the international stage. Crosby, like all the other Canadian players, had to go through the selection camp, but there was never any question in the mind of Hockey Canada general manager Steve Yzerman that the Penguins superstar would be part of Team Canada in Vancouver. At the orientation camp over the summer, Crosby, fresh off a Cup win, did not miss a step in the practice sessions. He impressed Team Canada's head coach Mike Babcock of the Detroit Red Wings, the same coach whose team he and the Penguins had just trounced in the Stanley Cup finals.

"He did a real good job in the playoffs," said Babcock. "I thought, in particular, Crosby's battle with [Henrik] Zetterburg was really good."

The official announcement of the team came on December 30, 2009, and sure enough, Crosby was at the top of Yzerman's wish list. But Crosby's Olympic experience had begun a month earlier when the Torch Relay entered his home province of Nova Scotia. The torch had traveled from the site of the ancient Olympics in Olympia, Greece, to the shores of Halifax, Nova Scotia. There, the province's favorite son took some time out of his NHL schedule to carry the torch on November 18, 2009, a once-in-a-lifetime experience.

"I am honored and thrilled to have the opportunity to carry the Olympic flame in my home province of Nova Scotia," Crosby said in a release to the media.

The night of Crosby's run with the torch, Halifax police shut down the city center where he would be running to accommodate the crowds that were guaranteed to show up every time their boy returned home. In the end, some 20,000 people came simply to see Crosby running with the Olympic flame.

The crowd was almost too large for Brunswick Street, and as Crosby's run came to an end and he handed off the flame to snowboarder Sarah Conrad, a security team converged on him to whisk him away from the ever-encroaching fans. It was a little disconcerting for the hockey superstar, but he took it all in stride because he understands the public's passion for the game and for the Olympics.

With the men's Olympic hockey roster set in stone, and the months of speculation at an end, Crosby and the rest of the team could focus their efforts on winning gold. But winning an Olympic gold medal in hockey for Canada, even on home ice, is not an easy task. No one wanted a repeat of the disappointing showing at the 2006 Turin Games, when the Canadian men were knocked out of the medals early in the tournament. After all, hockey *is* Canada's game, and the entire country expected our NHL-level players to win.

The task of assembling a squad fell to Steve Yzerman, who took over the job from Wayne Gretzky in 2007. Gretzky had started his term as Team Canada's general manager by bringing home gold from the 2002 Salt Lake City games (Canada's first in 50 years). But in 2006, the Canadian men fell apart and were sent home early from the Olympics with heads hanging low. The players from 2006, such as Todd Bertuzzi and Ryan Smyth, were rough-and-tumble veterans, highly skilled but not necessarily equipped for an international hockey tournament that has begun to turn more and more into a youth movement. Although Crosby was only 19 years old in 2006, many sports writers suggested that he be placed on the Olympic team, but Gretzky felt the young forward was not yet ready for such pressures. When the announcement came that Yzerman would take over the helm of our hockey hopes, he decided that it was time to hand over the future of Canadian hockey to younger players such as Drew Doughty, Duncan Keith, Jonathan Toews and, of course, Sidney Crosby. Yzerman would add 2006 veterans Chris Pronger, Scott Niedermayer and Jarome Iginla to round out the team, but the flavor of the group was definitely looking toward the future.

The country waited with bated breath for the Olympics to begin. And while everyone watched as athletes like Alexandre Bilodeau won Canada's first gold medal on home soil in the freestyle moguls competition and cried along with Joannie Rochette when her mother died just days before her Olympic figure skating performance, it was the men's hockey team that had the nation glued to their seats.

The favorites going into the games were surprisingly not the Canadians but the speedy, skilled Russians led by Alexander Ovechkin. Even before the tournament began, sports pundits were already talking of the two hockey powers facing off in the final for the gold. But considering all the other countries involved, the Swedes were always a force to be reckoned with, and the U.S. could also surprise given their speed up front with players such as Phil Kessel and Zach Parise. The Canadians were expected to go far, but after 2006, no one was taking anything for granted.

Arriving 24 hours before the start of their first game against Norway, Crosby and the rest of team had little time to acclimatize to their surroundings and only managed to get in one 35-minute practice session before being thrown into the tournament on February 16, 2010. When the Canadian team stepped onto the ice, the roar from the crowd matched the level of a jet engine, leaving a few of the players, Crosby included, a little nervous at the start of the game. Those nerves were apparent in the opening minutes of the first period. Crosby looked out of step with his line mates, sending a few passes off the mark, and the first period ended with no goals.

Canadian head coach Mike Babcock knew he needed to shake things up in order to get the players flowing out on the ice and shaking off their nerves. After some inspiring words, he made a few alterations to the lines, putting Crosby with Jarome Iginla and Rick Nash. It was a combination he had tried during summer training camp but had changed when the three did not click right away. Just two and a half minutes into the second frame while on the power play, Iginla took a perfect feed from Crosby and wired the first goal of the tournament past the Norwegian goaltender. The goal gave the Canadians the boost they needed, and they went on to win the game by a convincing score of 8–0. Crosby finished with three assists.

The younger players on the team were brimming with confidence after the win, but the veterans knew that the gold medal game was a long way away. Sensing trouble on the horizon in their next game against Switzerland, team captain Scott Niedermayer canceled a planned team trip to another event at the Games and replaced it with a team planning session and optional practice. It would be too easy for the young players, even cool customers like Crosby, to get caught up in the hype surrounding the team and the Games.

The veteran's intuition proved true when Team Canada hit the ice two days later against the Swiss and their hot goaltender, Jonas Hiller. Canada was the first to open up the scoring on a goal by Dany Heatley at the 9:21 mark of the first period and potted another in the opening of the second on a goal by Patrick Marleau. The score was 2–0, but if not for the spectacular goaltending of Jonas Hiller, Canada would have had a far bigger lead. At the end of two periods, they had blasted 27 shots in his direction, and not one was an easy save. Hiller's heroics did not go unnoticed by his teammates, who battled tenaciously and managed to scored two second-period goals to tie the game. The third period solved nothing, and neither did overtime, so the game would be decided by an always-exciting shootout.

Hiller and Brodeur each stopped the first three attempts on goal that the opposing team sent down the ice. In the NHL, sending another player out again to shoot is not allowed, but International Ice Hockey Federation rules allow a team to choose any shooter it likes for the tiebreaker.

So on a gut feeling, Babcock sent Crosby for his second shot of the night. This time he made no mistake, faking with his shoulder to freeze Hiller, ,then burying a wrist shot on the low stick side.

"You know what, we didn't take them lightly," said Crosby in an interview immediately after the game. "I don't think we came in here expecting an easy game, and we didn't get one. We had the right intentions, but it's still early, and we need to work some kinks out here, but we have to continue to improve."

Wise words from Crosby, since Team Canada's next opponents would provide them with their greatest challenge of the tournament. Not getting full points for their shootout win against the Swiss, Canada needed to beat their next opponents in the final game of the round robin pool, or they would have to play an extra game to qualify for the quarterfinals. Their next challenger would be the United States.

When it comes to hockey and the United States, there is one emotion the majority of Canadians feel—hatred. Outside the arena, Canadians for the most part are friendly toward our neighbors to the south, but when it comes to our national sport/religion, all the smiles and kind words go out the door. For Canadians, this is war. Many thought that defeating the Americans in the

Olympics would be sweet revenge for what the U.S. Junior team had done to the Canadians a month earlier by taking the championship in the World Junior gold medal finals.

Normally, Americans hardly care enough to posture before a big hockey game, but this time, Team USA forward Ryan Kesler, who plays for the Vancouver Canucks, sat in front of reporters before the game and fired the first salvo on the subject of Canadians. "I hate them," he said, before backtracking. "It's a big rivalry. Obviously, Canadians, it's their game. I wouldn't say 'I hate them.' You have respect for the other team. But Canadians expect to win gold, and anything less is not good enough. It's going to be fun to try to knock them off."

The Canadian players refused to comment on Kessler's comments, or anything else related to the American players, preferring to remain focused on the game ahead. However, remaining stoic in the face of the brash Americans didn't work. Just 41 seconds into the game, Brian Rafalaski scored on a shot that deflected off Crosby's leg and past goaltender Martin Brodeur. Eric Staal then tied the game up around the halfway mark of the period, but just a minute later, Rafalaski scored again to put the Americans ahead. The two teams then traded goals, giving the Americans a 3–2 lead at the end of the second period.

At the seven-minute mark of the third, it seemed the game might be over when the Americans scored again to make it 4–2, but Sidney Crosby stepped up and gave the his team some hope, scoring a goal with just over three minutes left in the game.

With that boost, the Canadians poured on the pressure in the dying minutes of the game, even pulling Brodeur to get the extra attacker, but Ryan Kesler managed to slip a puck into the empty cage for the killer blow. For the fans in attendance and for the millions of Canadians watching at home, it was a devastating loss. But it was not the end of the world. Crosby and the Canadians would simply have to defeat the Germans to gain entrance into the quarterfinals. That game was a breeze for the Canadian men, with Crosby coming out with a goal and a couple of assists for an 8–2 victory over Germany.

Defeating the Germans was almost a foregone conclusion, but the loss to the Americans had shattered Canadians' unflappable belief in their team's ability to win gold. Their next opponents would not make that feeling go away.

The Russian team was a formidable bunch on paper, led by Crosby's nemesis, Alexander Ovechkin, and solid players such as Pavel Datsyuk and veteran defenseman Sergei Gonchar.

But unlike the Canadians, the Russians had not been able to play a team game since the start of the tournament. So Team Canada took advantage of their weakness. However, it was not the Crosby–Ovechkin matchup the world had been waiting for in the weeks leading up to the Games—both players were held off the scoresheet. It was Crosby's teammates that picked up the slack, scoring seven goals to the Russians' three, thereby winning a berth in the semifinals against the Slovaks. Despite Team Canada's success, the media reported that Crosby had so far under-performed in the Olympics. Some feared the pressure was too great for the young superstar, who was being watched by eyes across the globe. But as Crosby has always proven throughout his hockey career, he can maintain a level head and deliver when the moment is right.

The Canadians managed to defeat a tough Slovak squad backstopped by the brilliant goaltending of Jaroslav Halak. Crosby was again held off the scoresheet, but that didn't matter. The victory meant the Canadians would move on to the gold medal final and would get a chance at redemption against the Americans.

Game Day. February 28, 2010.

Across Canada, all anyone could talk about was the gold medal game. Up to that point in the

Olympics, Canada as a nation had won an incredible 13 gold medals, tying the record for the most gold medals won in a Winter Olympics by one country. A win at the men's hockey final would give Canada a record-breaking performance and at the same time whip the country into a patriotic frenzy. Around downtown Vancouver and all across the country, fans were sitting in front of giant screens and televisions, waiting for the opening puck to drop. Inside Canada Hockey Place, a sea of red and white filled the arena, and the atmosphere was electric. One young woman even held up a sign that read, "Sid, Check Out My Soft Hands." Prime Minister Steven Harper was in attendance, as were other notables such as William Shatner and Michael J. Fox. But if the people in the arena and the country were nervous before the game, the players were feeling the pressure tenfold. But this was destiny—on home ice at the Olympics. It had to be...Right?

At the drop of the puck, it was easy to see that both the Canadians and the Americans were feeling the collective weight of their country's expectations. Neither side played its system, and as a result, in the first five minutes, both teams had golden opportunities to open the scoring, but Canadian goaltender Roberto Luongo and U.S. goaltender Ryan Miller were up to the task. Finally, after 12 agonizing minutes, Jonathan

Toews scored to put Canada up 1–0, sending the crowd into a frenzy. Corey Perry put Canada up by two when he buried a rebound in behind Miller for a seemingly insurmountable lead. Crosby had a few chances on goal in the first two periods, but he couldn't get anything past Miller. After the quick lead, Canada appeared to become complacent, allowing Ryan Kesler to put the Americans within one goal. The late goal gave the Americans the boost they needed in the third period, and Team USA completely dominated the Canadians, forcing plays and keeping the puck deep in the zone. Luckily Luongo held firm, and with the clock slowly ticking down, it appeared that Canada might just squeeze by for the win. But then Ryan Miller was pulled in favor of an extra attacker, and all hell broke loose. With the puck deep in the Canadian zone, U.S. forward Patrick Kane took a desperation shot that deflected out into the open, where Zach Parise simply pushed it past Luongo with only 24 seconds left on the clock.

Thirty-three million people across Canada and countless numbers around the globe were suddenly drained of all joy. On the Canadian bench, elation evaporated, leaving a gut-wrenching feeling instead. To get the game back, *someone* would have to score in four-on-four overtime.

In overtime, both sides traded a few chances, but neither wanted to make a mistake and let the gold medal slip through their fingers. Crosby had been relatively absent on the scoresheet throughout the tournament and had been criticized for not stepping up when it mattered most. But all questions surrounding Crosby's play vanished in one brilliant flash of a stick.

Seven and a half minutes into the overtime period, Crosby broke into the American's zone and tried to split the defense. Ryan Miller pushed the puck into the corner, only to have Crosby pick it up again. He tried to carry it along the boards, but when the puck got caught in the skates of the referee, Crosby had to push it into the corner toward Iginla. Seeing an opening in front of the net, Crosby suddenly took off, leaving behind his defensive coverage. He screamed, "Iggy!!" to get the puck back. Iginla managed to break past defenseman Ryan Suter, falling to his knees to get the puck back onto Crosby's stick. Crosby then moved the puck from his backhand to his forehand and took a quick shot that caught Ryan Miller off guard. The puck slipped through a space between Miller's legs and into the net for the win.

"I wasn't really aiming for anything," Crosby said immediately after the game. "I didn't see it go into the net. I just heard everyone screaming."

Once he knew the puck had found its mark, Crosby leapt into the air, throwing off his gloves and sending his stick flying. His teammates instantly mobbed him. In Canada, you could almost feel a wave of energy being released all at once across the country as 33 million people suddenly came to life after sitting on tenterhooks for those last tense seven and a half minutes.

Crosby had been criticized for his lack of effort, but when team and country needed him the most, he stepped forward with a goal that will surely rank as one of the greatest in Canadian hockey history, right along side Paul Henderson's in the 1972 Summit Series. Not only did the goal give Team Canada a gold medal, but it also gave Canada the record for the most gold medals won at a Winter Olympics with 14.

After the obligatory handshakes, Crosby lined up for the medal ceremony, and when it came time for Olympic president Jacques Rogge to place the medal around Crosby's neck, the crowd began chanting, "Crosby! Crosby! Crosby!" only to be encouraged further by the IOC president to chant louder. Crosby naturally tried to remain humble, but there was no stopping the crowd. He was their hero. He was Canada's hero.

The weight of an entire nation suddenly melted away with a single goal. Crosby knew that he could have played better during the tournament. Even general manager Steve Yzerman gave a mediocre assessment of his play after the gold medal game, "He was great at times, and other times good." But that single moment was for the country to cherish.

Once the parties and celebrations died down, Crosby wanted to move on and focus his energy

Chapter Fourteen

Back to Reality

on the regular NHL season. There was, after all, another Stanley Cup to go after.

After taking only a few days to recover mentally and physically from the pressure and adrenaline of the Olympics, Sidney Crosby was back in Pittsburgh. Many expected the young Nova Scotia native to be a little sluggish in his first few games back with the team, but he picked up right where he left off, scoring goals.

The Penguins once again finished the season near the top of the standings with 101 points, good enough for fourth place in the Eastern Conference. For his part, Crosby finished the season with 109 points, not a personal best, but it was his 51 goals (a career high) that won him the Maurice Rocket Richard Trophy, although he had to share it with Steven Stamkos of the Tampa Bay Lightning.

"One of the guys on the bench told me Stamkos had scored," Crosby said after the last game of the season in which he scored his 51st goal. "There's a little bit of healthy competition there, and we all know that for the last week or so there has been a bit of a race. I tried to leave it out there and see where it brought me. It's never easy to tie, but I'll take the tie on this one."

It was a nice achievement, but more importantly, the Penguins were in a good position going into the playoffs. And their captain was scoring goals.

In the playoffs, the Penguins were able to defeat the Ottawa Senators in the opening round. Crosby was the dominant player on the ice, scoring five goals. But it was his performance in game two that was the talk of the hockey world for that series. He scored one goal, completely dominated on both ends of the rink and delivered one of the most inspiring performances, assisting Kris Letang on the game-winning goal. Hanging onto the puck behind the Ottawa net and with Ottawa forward Jason Spezza chasing him, Crosby skated back and forth below the goal line, looking for an opportunity. The way he protected the puck made Spezza look like a rookie, and then Crosby managed to make a crisp pass to Letang for the goal. It was another virtuoso performance for the player who never stops surprising.

"I was just trying to get some space," said Crosby after that game. "Someone was on me, not sure who was following me around, they were tracking me pretty good. I just tried to make a play to Tanger [Letang]. He had a ton of time. He did a great job getting through. They had a lot of guys there."

After handing Ottawa their pass to the golf course, next up for Crosby was the Montreal Canadiens, who had just come off a series with the Washington Capitals. The Canadiens had finished in the eighth and final playoff spot, and not one person in the hockey world had predicted they could defeat the mighty Washington Capitals. But on the strength of their defensive system and the brilliant goaltending of Jaroslav Halak, the Canadiens managed to win in the seventh game and move on to face the Penguins.

The Canadiens were, of course, the team that had drafted Sidney Crosby's father almost three decades earlier, and they were the team that he had grown up cheering for. But none of that mattered now; he wanted to win.

Pittsburgh opened up the series with an easy 6–3 win over a tired-looking Canadiens team. After that performance, it appeared that the Penguins would have no trouble with Montreal, but the Cinderella team of the playoffs wasn't finished surprising. Montreal employed the same strategy they'd used against the Capitals in shutting down the top offensive players. All Crosby could manage was one goal in the entire series that went all the way to game seven. And the Penguins ended up losing in front of a hometown crowd. They were frustrated throughout the Montreal series and could not seem to solve goaltender Jaroslav Halak.

And it just so happened that it was the last game the Penguins would play inside the old Mellon Arena. In a strange twist of irony, the Montreal Canadiens was the team the Penguins had first played there in 1967. The Penguins had lost both games to the Habs.

Crosby, for his part, was frustrated by his team's performance on the ice and dismissed claims that he was overtired because of the long playoffs the year before and the Olympics.

"I'm not going to sit here and complain about playing Stanley Cup finals and Olympic gold medal games," he said after the game seven loss to the Canadiens. "That's a good problem to have, and you have to deal with it. There are times when it is a grind, and you have to deal with it. By no means is that any excuse or any reason for anything. It's definitely disappointing. Game seven, anything can happen and, unfortunately, we weren't [at] our best."

All in all, it was a pretty successful year for the young superstar, but after all the attention and work he had put in, a summer off to relax was the best thing for him. He had been through the most incredible two years of his young career, living up to his own and everyone else's expectations. And while the world awaits his next incredible exploits on the ice, in true Canadian fashion, he carries all these pressures with humility and good nature.

Chapter Fifteen

Quotes, Quips, Quiz and Quick Facts on Sidney Crosby

Quotations About or From Sidney Crosby

I'm not trying to be the next Wayne Gretzky or Mario Lemieux....I am putting pressure on myself to do my best and perform to my potential—that's all I can do.

–Sidney Crosby

It means a lot to us, to the league and to Rimouski. We are very proud to have him in our league.

–Gilles Corteaun, QMJHL Commissioner

I don't think there's ever a time where I step back and say I wish I was something different. I'm doing what I love to do.

–Sidney Crosby

I looked forward to it for a long time. It feels awesome. Yeah, I was happy. It's something you dream of, scoring in the NHL, and you only

*do it the first time once. It was big. There's a lot
of emotion. The fans were great. It was so loud. I
never expected to hear them [chanting] my
name. You never expect that.*
–Sidney Crosby

*I'd love to have the opportunity to do that....
Obviously I'm going to be a rookie, so I'm going
to try to learn as much as a I can, be open-
minded. And be a student...I'm going to learn
from one of the best guys in Mario Lemieux. So
I'm going to try and be a sponge in that way
and learn as much as I can from him.*
–Sidney Crosby, on getting to learn from the Pittsburgh Penguins greatest player in his rookie year

*I want to be the best. So whatever comes with
that, I have to accept it.*
–Sidney Crosby

*I realize there will not be another Gretzky, and
I will be the first one to say I will not break his
records....But for him to say that I could, it
means I am doing something right. It was probably the best compliment I could get. I'm going
to remember it.*
–Sidney Crosby

*My dad introduced me to the game, gave me
a stick. Since then I've had a passion for it.*
–Sidney Crosby

You can see the talent is there. I don't know if you got a true vision of him tonight. It's tough to play your first NHL game.

–New Jersey Devils coach Larry Robinson, on Crosby's first game

I haven't changed one bit; I never dove, and I don't dive now…That's just part of the play-offs; part of gamesmanship. If I go down, it's because I've been forced down. I'll do whatever I can to stay on my feet. I think he [Renney] should be the one worried about diving.

–Sidney Crosby, on accusations by New York Rangers head coach Tom Renney that Crosby was taking dives during the 2008 playoff eastern semifinal

Crosby, in large part because his father Troy was drafted by the team, was always a big Montreal Canadiens fan. Prior to the 2005 entry draft, it was widely assumed he would have liked to have been drafted by the Canadiens. Now 19, Crosby will be eligible for free agency when he turns 25, at which point he can sign with any team. He has never come right out and said it specifically, but I have no doubt in my mind that he would one day like to play for the Montreal Canadiens. I think it would mean a lot to him. I think he has a lot of love for the city of Montreal.

–Shawna Richer, in her book, *A Season with Sidney Crosby in the NHL*

*I think he has a moat around his house with
a dragon guarding the front gate. The guy
is a legend. He's the only guy in the world with
a dragon. I think Tim Hortons hired a dragon
to guard him.*

–Pittsburgh Penguin teammate Colby
Armstrong, on Sidney Crosby

*I want to make the world juniors team and play
against a lot of world-class teams. It was heart-
breaking last year, and I definitely want to do
it again.*

–Sidney Crosby, on his experiences at the
World Junior tournaments

I've accomplished a lot for being 16.

–Sidney Crosby

*No special treatment at home. He has a little
sister he has to fight over the TV with.*

–Troy Crosby, on his son's rise to fame

*Being Canadian, you want to play for Team
Canada. With the talent that Canada has, they
always have a chance to win. It would be nice
to be part of that.*

–Sidney Crosby, on participating in the
2010 Olympics

Our savior has arrived.

–Sign held by unidentified
Pittsburgh Penguins' fan

It's hard to compare, because you look at his size, there were players of his size [in the past]. But work like he works, they will not.

–Minnesota Wild coach Jacques Lemaire, on Sidney Crosby's potential for greatness, while using the grammar of Master Yoda, "But work like he works, they will not. YES!"

I have been practicing since I was four or five years old, but that wasn't really practice. I was just having fun....I just loved to play hockey.

–Sidney Crosby

Well, on a day like today, you know, you remember the early mornings. Definitely I can remember they had to take on an extra job just so I could keep playing hockey. We did things just like that so I could continue to play a game I love. This is something I guess that makes them realize it was worth it, to see me have the opportunity to play in the NHL.

–Sidney Crosby, on the role of his parents in his hockey career

For every whack I've given, I've gotten four or five.

–Sidney Crosby

It's not that hard to stay grounded. It's the way I was brought up.

–Sidney Crosby, on responding to the pressure

It's difficult because you get people coming to your house, strangers, knocking on the door. Sometimes it's unnerving, you get phone calls from strangers.

–Troy Crosby, on his son's fame

I need to work on defensive play and being consistent.

–Sidney Crosby, on the aspects of his game

The speed of the game is something he'll have to adjust to.

–Mario Lemieux, on Sidney Crosby at the
2005 NHL Entry Draft

No!

–Mario Lemieux, when a reporter asked him if
the 17-year-old Sidney Crosby might be sent back
down to the minors

I didn't anticipate anything—I was just showing up and seeing what the town and people were about, but it was a very welcoming sight.…I'm sure the energy and excitement in town are going to rub off on the players. It's nice to see everybody's so excited about getting hockey started.

–Sidney Crosby

He keeps you on the edge of your seat. He gets off the ice, and you can't wait to see him get back on.

–Former NHL star Gilles Meloche

*An 18-year-old kid says he's going to give us
ideas. What, from the Quebec League, he's going
to give them ideas? Come on. That's ridiculous.*
> –Don Cherry, after Sidney Crosby was named
> alternate Pittsburgh Penguins captain

*No kid should have as much a say as he's got to
say, yapping at the referees, doing the whole
thing, golden boy. This kid has really taken over
the whole thing.*
> –Don Cherry, criticizing Crosby for his
> on-ice antics

*He said he needs to work on his shot a little bit.
But it looks pretty good to me.*
> –Hockey legend Mario Lemieux

*I've won the Stanley Cup, won gold medals.
Getting Sidney Crosby was the happiest day of
my life.*
> –Penguins executive Craig Patrick, on winning
> the draft lottery and selecting Sidney Crosby

*You're not going to intimidate this kid. He's not
going to back off. There are players like that.
When we played against Henri Richard or
Frank Mahovlich, the word at our meetings was
leave those guys alone. Ask them how their families are doing, but don't wake them up. If you
tick them off, they become even better players.*
> –Penguins executive Ed Johnston

We have a very strong idea of being grounded. We understand the real world and how it works.

> –Trina Crosby, Sidney's mother

I've seen a lot of kids come and go. This kid gets it. He's a special kid, but he gets it.

> –Gord Cutler, veteran NHL producer

I haven't won the Stanley Cup yet, so ask me after that. But this has been a couple of memorable weeks.

> –Sidney Crosby, after winning the Hart Trophy, the Lester Pearson Trophy and the Art Ross Trophy at the 2007 NHL Awards

Hey Sidney, put it in my five-hole.

> –A sign held up by a female fan of the young superstar Sidney Crosby

He is the best hockey player in the world. Everybody is excited for the chance to play with him.

> –Jarome Iginla, on his chance to play with Crosby during the Vancouver 2010 Olympic Winter Games.

It's a dream come true to win a gold medal. To score in overtime, here in Canada, what's better than that? I've dreamed of that moment a thousand times.

> –Sidney Crosby, moments after winning the gold for Canada at the Vancouver 2010 Olympics

It would've been nice to keep things going, but it was one of those games. It's always easy to look back. I just try to go out there and do the same things.
  –Sidney Crosby, after the New York Islanders put an end to his point-scoring streak at 25 games during the 2010–11 season

I learned just to keep an open mind about everything and to not get too caught up in everything. You're better off expecting to have to adjust. It's a big event. It's just a different look. I remember in Buffalo it was just starting to get dark when we were finishing. But this one will be different and probably a neat feeling.
  –Sidney Crosby, on the 2011 Winter Classic game against the Washington Capitals

The Crosby Quiz

Q: Why does Sidney Crosby wear the number 87 on his jersey?

A: Crosby chose to wear the number 87 because he was born in the eighth month on the seventh day in 1987.

Q: What was Sidney Crosby's favorite NHL team growing up?

A: Sidney Crosby was a big fan of the Montreal Canadiens, as were many East Coast inhabitants, but he had another reason to cheer for the Canadiens. They were his father's favorite team and the club that had selected him 240th overall in the 1984 draft.

Q: Whom did Sidney Crosby first live with when he played in his rookie season with the Pittsburgh Penguins?

A: Because Crosby was still a teenager and a rookie, Mario Lemieux took the young Sidney into his home in Pittsburgh, and Sidney even relied on the Penguins captain and owner to drive him to and from practice.

Q: What did Sidney Crosby use as target practice in his parents' basement?

A: Crosby spent hours in the basement putting many dents in his parents' dryer. The young

Crosby, who spent countless hours working on his aim, covered nearly every inch of the dryer in black puck marks. Considering the way the dryer looks, it took many years to perfect.

Q: What team and what goaltender did Sidney Crosby score his first NHL goal against?

A: In his third game of his rookie season in 2005–06, Sidney Crosby scored his first NHL goal on October 8, 2005, against Boston Bruins goaltender Hannu Toivonen.

Q: Who was chosen second overall after Sidney Crosby at the 2005 NHL Entry Draft?

A: American-born forward Bobby Ryan was selected second overall behind Sidney Crosby by the Anaheim Mighty Ducks.

Q: What was significant about Sidney Crosby becoming captain of the Pittsburgh Penguins in May 2007?

A: In May 2007, Sidney Crosby was still just 19 years old, thus making him the youngest ever captain in the history of the NHL.

Q: What number did Crosby always try to wear before turning pro, and why?

A: It was Maurice Richard's number; Gordie Howe had it on the back of his jersey; and

Bobby Hull scored over 600 goals with it. All these players wore the number 9 on their jerseys, and Sidney Crosby, always wanting to emulate the best, tried whenever possible to have the number 9 on his jersey.

Bonus Questions

Q: Where did Sidney get the nickname Darryl?

A: During Sidney's first exhibition game with the Rimouski Oceanic in 2004, he scored eight points. His teammates started calling him Darryl from then on, in reference to Darryl Sittler of the NHL, who scored 10 points in one game.

Q: How long did Sidney Crosby's personal record-setting scoring streak last during the 2010–11 NHL season?

A: Over 25 straight games, Crosby kept fans on the edge of their seats. Not since the 1992–93 season, when Mats Sundin went 30 straight games with a point, has the league seen anything like it. And who better to keep the crowds cheering than Sidney Crosby. His accomplishment was amazing but nowhere near the incredible record set by Wayne Gretzky during the 1983–84 season, when he went 51 consecutive games with a point or more.

Q: Did Sidney Crosby get a point in the 2011
   Winter Classic outdoor game versus the Washington Capitals?

A: No. He was held pointless through the game.
   The Penguins lost 3–1. Evgeni Malkin scored
   the lone Pittsburgh goal with assists from Kris
   Letang and Marc-Andre Fleury.

Crosby Quick Facts

- Like most players, Sidney Crosby has his own set of superstitions before a game. He always puts on his right-side equipment first, eats at the same time before a game, always goes to bed at the same time before a game, and does not let anyone touch his sticks before a game.

- In the basement of Mario Lemieux's Pittsburgh home, there is a picture on the wall of a young Mario Lemieux scoring a top-shelf goal on Troy Crosby when both of them played junior hockey in Quebec.

- Sidney has a younger sister named Taylor

- Crosby shoots from the left

- Height: 5 feet 11 inches;
  Weight: 200 pounds

- Favorite player growing up: Steve Yzerman

- Pittsburgh Penguins teammate Evgeni Malkin was surprised to see captain Sidney Crosby use his slap shot during the 2008 Stanley Cup playoffs and joked with reporters after the game that Crosby had one of the weaker shots on the team.

- Placed thirty-fourth in the Askmen.com Top 49 Men of 2007

- Favorite pre-game meal: spaghetti

- Nominee for the 2007 and 2008 *Time* magazine list of the 100 Most Influential People

- Sixth place in *The Wall Street Journal*'s Top Ten World's Greatest Athletes. The NHL star combines stamina, power and the coordination to shoot a puck while getting clobbered. Panelists said hockey requires a level of endurance and strength that would put any golfer to shame.

- Sidney Crosby was the stick boy at the 2002 World Junior Championships.

- Few know that Sidney Crosby is not just an incredible hockey player but that his talents also extend to the baseball diamond. In 1998, Crosby won the Atlantic Canadian baseball championship with the Cole Harbour Cardinals, and he continued to play while at Shattuck–St. Mary's. Crosby's position of choice was pitcher. While at Shattuck, he and fellow hockey defenseman Jack Johnson were an equally skilled team on the diamond as on the ice.

  "I wasn't very good, but Sidney was actually a really good baseball player," Johnson said. "He was pitching, and the other team's pitcher was giving him a hard time from the bench because Sidney was having a really good game. Sidney was sick of it, and I said, 'Don't worry, I'll take care of it.' I went up and crowded the plate so he'd hit me and give me a reason to go after him. So I took off when he hit me."

- At 18 years of age, Crosby signed a multi-million dollar endorsement deal with Reebok.

- He also has endorsement deals with Gatorade and Tim Hortons.

- The day Crosby played his first NHL game on October 5, 2005, was also Mario Lemieux's 40th birthday.

- Sidney Crosby's nicknames: The Next One, Darryl, Sid the Kid and Sir Sidney

- Crosby was named a member of Canada's National Ice Hockey team for the 2010 Vancouver Olympics.

- Before Crosby, the youngest captain to win the Stanley Cup was Mike Grant of the 1895 Montreal Victorias, who was 21 years and 2 months old when he hoisted the Cup.

- Sidney Crosby, he is a creature of habit. Most hockey players are like that, but Crosby has taken the practice to the extreme, especially when it comes to one piece of his equipment. Without a doubt, his most cherished piece of gear is his jockstrap. He has been wearing the same one since before he even joined the Rimouski Oceanique. Equipment managers with the Pittsburgh Penguins have been given specific instructions not to replace the jock despite its dirty, tattered appearance, and when it rips, they just sew it right up again. It might be a little gross, but you can't argue with Crosby's performance on the ice. As long as he keeps scoring, he can keep wearing the dirty jock.

• In December 2010, Sidney Crosby, Alexander Ovechkin and former NHLer Jeremy Roenick appeared on an episode of the famous U.S. television show *The Price is Right*. They were on set to introduce an NHL-themed showcase that included a trip to Pittsburgh for the NHL Winter Classic. The package also included VIP passes to the NHL's New Year's Eve bash, ice-level access during the practices when the Penguins and the Capitals met on Heinz Field on December 31 and a 2011 Honda CR-Z hybrid.

- The Crosby Hat Trick—There is now a new hat trick to add to the two already well-known ones:

  -The Original Hat Trick, in which a player scores three goals in one game

  -The Gordie Howe Hat Trick, in which a player scores a goal, gets an assist and gets into a fight

  -The Crosby Hat Trick, in which a player scores a goal, gets an assist and makes a save

  During the 2010 Eastern Conference quarterfinals against the Ottawa Senators, Crosby scored in the first period, got an assist on the game-winning goal, and when Anton Volchenkov beat Penguins goaltender Marc-Andre Fleury with a slap shot, Crosby was posted along the goal line and was able to clear the puck, thus giving birth to the Crosby Hat Trick.

Stats on Sidney Crosby

Regular Season And Playoff Statistics

Season	Team	League	GP	G	A	PTS	PIM
2000–01 Regular Season	Cole Harbour Red Wings	Bantam AAA	63	86	96	182	0
2000–01 Playoffs	Cole Harbour Red Wings	Bantam AAA	5	10	6	16	0
2001–02 Regular Season	Dartmouth Subways	Midget AAA	74	95	98	193	114
2001–02 Playoffs	Dartmouth Subways	Midget AAA	7	11	13	24	0
2002–03 Regular Season	Shattuk St-Mary's	USHS	57	72	90	162	104
2002–03 Playoffs	Shattuk St-Mary's	USHS					
2003–04 Regular Season	Rimouski Oceanic	QMJHL	59	54	81	135	74
2003–04 Playoffs	Rimouski Oceanic	QMJHL	9	7	9	16	10
2004–05 Regular Season	Rimouski Oceanic	QMJHL	62	66	102	168	84
2004–05 Playoffs	Rimouski Oceanic	QMJHL	13	14	17	31	16
2005–06 Regular Season	Pittsburgh Penguins	NHL	81	39	63	102	110
2005–06 Playoffs	Pittsburgh Penguins	NHL					
2006–07 Regular Season	Pittsburgh Penguins	NHL	79	36	84	120	60
2006–07 Playoffs	Pittsburgh Penguins	NHL	5	3	2	5	4
2007–08 Regular Season	Pittsburgh Penguins	NHL	53	24	48	72	39

2007–08 Playoffs	Pittsburgh Penguins	NHL	20	6	21	27	12
2008–09 Regular Season	Pittsburgh Penguins	NHL	77	33	70	103	76
2008–09 Playoffs	Pittsburgh Penguins	NHL	24	15	16	31	14
2009–10 Regular Season	Pittsburgh Penguins	NHL	81	51	58	109	69
2009–10 Playoffs	Pittsburgh Penguins	NHL	13	6	13	19	6

International Statistics

Year	Team	Event	GP	G	A	PTS	PIM
2004	Team Canada	WJC	6	2	3	5	4
2005	Team Canada	WJC	6	6	3	9	4
2006	Team Canada	WC	8	8	16	10	0
2010	Team Canada	2010 Olympics	7	4	3	7	4

Legend

GP = Games Played

G = Goals

A = Assists

PTS = Points

PIM = Penalty Minutes

USHS = United States High School

WJC = World Junior Championship

WC = World Championship

Sidney Crosby Records

- Pittsburgh Penguins' franchise record for assists in a season by a rookie (63)

- Pittsburgh Penguins' franchise record for points in a season by a rookie (102)

- First rookie to record 100 points and 100 penalty minutes in a season

- Youngest player in NHL history to record 100 points in a season

- Youngest player in NHL history to record 200 career points (19 years, 207 days old)

- Youngest player in NHL history to have two consecutive 100-point seasons.

- Youngest player to be voted to the NHL All-Star Game

- Youngest player in NHL history to win the Art Ross Trophy

- Youngest player in NHL history to win the Lester B. Pearson Award

- Youngest player in NHL history to be named to the First All-Star Team

- Youngest player in NHL history to be named a full team captain (In January 1984, Brian Bellows of the Minnesota North Stars was made interim captain at five months younger than Crosby, but Bellows only served the latter half of the 1983–84 season, replacing injured captain Craig Hartsburg.)

- When the Pittsburgh Penguins won the 2009 Stanley Cup Championship, Sidney Crosby became the youngest captain to win the Cup. He was 21 years, 10 months and 5 days old.

Awards

Midget AAA

2002: National Championships Tournament Most Valuable Player Award

2002: National Championships Tournament Top Scorer Award

Quebec Major Junior Hockey League

2004: RDS/JVC Rookie of the Year Trophy

2004: QMJHL All-Rookie Team

2004: QMJHL First All-Star Team

2004, 2005: Michel Briere Trophy as QMJHL MVP

2004, 2005: Jean Beliveau Trophy as QMJHL Leading Scorer

2005: Mike Bossy Trophy as QMJHL best professional prospect

2004, 2005: Paul Dumont Trophy as QMJHL Personality of the Year

2005: Guy Lafleur Trophy as the QMJHL Playoff MVP

2004: Michel Bergeron Trophy as QMJHL Offensive Rookie of the Year

Canadian Hockey League

2004: CHL Rookie of the Year

2004, 2005: CHL Player of the Year

2004, 2005: CHL Leading Scorer

2004, 2005: Canada Post Cup

2005: Memorial Cup All-Star Team

2005: Ed Chynoweth Trophy (Memorial Cup Leading Scorer)

NHL

2007: Art Ross Trophy (most points in the regular season)

2007: Lester B. Pearson Award (best player as voted by his peers)

2007: Hart Memorial Trophy (most valuable player in the NHL)

2007: NHL first All-Star Team

2007: NHL All-Rookie Team

2007: Mark Messier Leadership Award

2009: Stanley Cup

2010: Mark Messier Leadership Award

2010: Maurice Rocket Richard Trophy

Winter Olympic Games

2010: Olympic Gold Medal

Other Awards

2007: Lou Marsh Trophy (Awarded to Canada's top athlete, professional or amateur)

2007: Lionel Conacher Award (Awarded to Canada's top male athlete of the year)

2007, 2008, 2009: ESPY Award for Best NHL Player

2008: The Order of Nova Scotia

2009: Lou Marsh Trophy

2009: Lionel Conacher Award

2010: ESPY Award for Best NHL Player

Notes on Sources

Book Sources

Arseneault, Paul, with Paul Hollingsworth. *Sidney Crosby: A Hockey Story*. Halifax: Nimbus Publishing, 2008.

Basu, Arpon. *Hockey's Hottest Players*. Montreal: OverTime Books, 2005.

Diamond, Dan, ed. *Total NHL*. Toronto: Dan Diamond and Associates, 2003.

Dixon, Ryan, and Ryan Kennedy. *Hockey's Young Guns: 25 Inside Stories on Making It to The Show*. Toronto: Transcontinental Publishing, 2007.

Goyens, Chrys, and Frank Orr. *Mario Lemieux: Over Time*. New York: Universe Publishing, 2001.

Joyce, Gare. *Sidney Crosby: Taking the Game by Storm*. Markham: Fitzhenry & Whiteside, 2007.

Podnieks, Andrew. *The Spectacular Sidney Crosby*. Bolton: Fenn Publishing, 2005.

Richer, Shawna. *The Rookie*. Toronto: McClelland & Stewart, 2006.

Web Sources

Wikipedia, the free encyclopedia (n.d.). en.wikipedia.org. Retrieved May 30 to July 15, 2008.

The Internet Hockey Database (n.d.). www.hockeydb.com. Retrieved May 30 to July 15, 2008.

TSN (n.d.). www.tsn.ca. Retrieved May 30 to July 15, 2008.

NHL (n.d.). www.nhl.com. Retrieved May 30 to July 15, 2008.

J. Alexander Poulton

J. Alexander Poulton is a writer and photographer and has been a genuine enthusiast of Canada's national pastime ever since seeing his first hockey game. His favorite memory is meeting the legendary gentleman hockey player Jean Béliveau, who in 1988 towered over the young awestruck author.

He earned his BA in English literature from McGill University and his graduate diploma in journalism from Concordia University. He has 25 other books to his credit, including *Canadian Hockey Record Breakers*, *Greatest Moments in Canadian Hockey*, and *Greatest Games of the Stanley Cup*, *Canadian Hockey Trivia*, *Hockey's Hottest Defensemen*, *The Montréal Canadiens*, *The Toronto Maple Leafs* and *A History of Hockey in Canada*.